1 Literacy Through Texts

Longman

Pearson Education Limited

Edinburgh Gate

Harlow

Essex

CM20 2JE

England and Associated Companies throughout the World

ISBN 0 582 43442 4

First published 2001

Second impression 2001

Reprinted 2001

Printed in Great Britain by Scotprint, Haddington

The Publisher's policy is to use paper manufactured from sustainable forests

Designed and packaged by McLean Press Limited

Cover illustration by Bee Willey

Illustrations by: Nick Schon (pages 5, 19, 20); Ros Hudson (pages 21, 22, 24); Lisa Smith (pages 25–34); Kristine Nason (pages 37–43); Tim Gaudion (pages 54–9); Ian Bosworth (pages 64–5); Gino D'Achille (pages 62, 67–73); Antonia Enthoven (page 79); Lynne Willey (pages 86–105); David Kearney (page 108); Colin Sullivan (pages 110–17); Chris Mould (pages 122–7); Nicola Evans (pages 129–35); Jamel Akib (pages 137–43); David Frankland (pages 144–8); Yvonne Muller (pages 157, 192–6); Nick Spender (pages 160, 165–8, 170–1); Diana Mayo (pages 172, 174); Sally Hynard (pages 175–7); Beryl Sanders (pages 178–89); John Haslam (page 198); Paul Thomas (page 199); Anne Wilson (pages 202–3); Ron Tiner (pages 205–13); Bee Willey (pages 214–16); Eric Robson (pages 224, 226–8, 231–5); Charlotte Combe (pages 3, 237); Rosemary Woods (pages 244–50, 252–3); Sally Taylor (page 254).

1

Literacy
Through Texts

Andrew Bennett
Jim Taylor

Contents

1 Just as I am

This chapter is about people and families: both in real life and in books. You will think about questions such as:

- What are these people like?
- How do I know?
- How do writers create characters?
- How can I tell fact from **fiction**?

Fiction is something which is invented or made-up by the writer. In a fiction text the writer may:
- make up everything, or
- set the text in a real place and involve some real people, but invent what happens.

Non-fiction is writing which deals with **facts**, such as a set of instructions, a travel guide or an account of a historic or scientific event. You need to read non-fiction with care because writers sometimes find it difficult to hide their opinions even when writing about facts!

Fiction texts

1 What would you expect to read about in a fiction **narrative**? *Hint: Think about some of the fiction you have read. Think about character, setting and plot.*

2 How would you expect a fiction narrative to be written? *Hint: Think about description and dialogue.*

3 What would make you want to keep on reading a long story?

1.1 Poetry and fiction

In the first section of this chapter, you will read prose fiction and poetry texts which describe people coping with a new arrival in the family – a baby – and the strong feelings that arouses.

Children on the Oregon Trail

The first text is part of a novel by the Dutch writer, A. Rutgers van der Loeff, *Children on the Oregon Trail*. It is based on the true story of thirteen-year-old John Sager who, with his family, was part of a wagon train of settlers heading for the far west of America in the summer of 1844.

As you read

Think about:

- why the Sager family decided to make such a dangerous journey

- what life on the trail was like, and how you might have felt in their situation

- how the writer keeps you interested and makes you wonder what is going to happen next.

A **narrative** is a text which tells a story. It may be in prose or poetry, and it may be fiction or it may include some information, like *Children on the Oregon Trail*.

Children on the Oregon Trail

That day began like any other.

At four o'clock in the morning, when the rising sun stood like a red-glowing ball above the grey landscape, the guards fired off their rifles, as a sign that the hours of sleep were past. Women, men, and children streamed out of every tent and wagon; the gently smouldering fires from the previous night were replenished with wood, and bluish-grey clouds from dozens of plumes of smoke began to float through the morning air. Bacon was fried, coffee was made, by those who still had some. The families which could still cook maize mush for the children thought themselves lucky.

All this took place within the 'corral', that was to say inside the ring which had been made by driving the wagons into a circle and fastening them firmly to each other by means of the shafts and chains. This formed a strong barricade through which even the most vicious ox could not break, and in the event of an attack by the Sioux Indians it would be a bulwark that was not to be despised.

Outside the corral the cattle and horses cropped the sparse grass in a wide circle.

At five o'clock sixty men mounted their horses and rode out of the camp. They fanned out through the crowds of cattle until they reached the outskirts of the herd; once there, they encircled the herd and began to drive all the cattle before them. The trained animals knew what those cracking whips meant, and what was required of them, and moved slowly in the direction of the camp. There the drivers picked their teams of oxen out from the dense mass and led them into the corral, where the yoke was put upon them.

From six o'clock until seven, the camp was extra busy; breakfast was eaten, tents were struck, wagons were loaded, and the teams of draught oxen and mules were made ready to be harnessed to their respective wagons and carts. Everyone knew that whoever was not ready when the signal to start was blown at seven o'clock would be doomed for that day to travel in the dusty rear of the caravan.

There were sixty-eight vehicles. They were divided into seventeen columns, each consisting of four wagons and carts. Each column took it in turn to lead the way. The section that was at the head today would bring up the rear tomorrow, unless a driver had missed his place in the row through laziness or negligence, and had to travel behind by way of punishment.

It was ten minutes to seven.

There were gaps everywhere in the corral; the teams of oxen were being harnessed in front of the wagons, the chains clanked. The women and children had taken their places under the canvas covers. The guide was standing among his assistants at the head of the line, ready to mount his horse and show the way. A dozen young men who were not on duty that day formed another group. They were going out buffalo-hunting; they had good horses and were well armed, which was certainly necessary, for the hostile Sioux had driven the herds of buffalo away from the River Platte, so that the hunters would be forced to ride fifteen or twenty miles to reach them.

As soon as the herdsmen were ready, they hurried to the rear of their herd, in order to drive them together and get them ready for today's march.

Seven o'clock.

An end had come to the busy running and walking to and fro, the cracking of whips, the shouts of command to the oxen, and the bawling from wagon to wagon – in short, to everything which, only just now, had appeared to be complete and utter chaos. Every driver was at his post. A bugle rang out! The guide and his escort mounted their horses; the four wagons of the leading section rumbled out of the camp and formed the first

column, the rest took their places with the regularity of clock-work, and the caravan moved slowly forward over the broad plateau, far above the foaming river.

A new, hard day had begun. Particularly hard for the Sagers, who were having to do without the help of Mrs Ford, since she had gone to look after Walton's sick child.

The sun rose high in the sky. It was hot and stuffy under the canvas tilts, which were thick with dust. Towards noon the children everywhere began to bicker and whimper. But in the Sager family's wagon, they had other things to worry about.

John, who had been riding for hours in the blazing sun, beside the heads of the foremost yoke of oxen, was given an order by his father, who was sitting on the driver's bench in the front of the wagon.

Immediately he galloped forward.

He had to fetch the doctor.

The doctor was a veterinary surgeon; the emigrants did not have a real doctor with them. But the vet had already done people a great deal of good, and helped them considerably, as well as animals.

John rode with all his might. Why on earth didn't the doctor travel in the middle of the caravan? From his father's face the boy had seen that the matter was urgent.

Meanwhile, Henry Sager had driven his wagon out of the line. He stopped.

'All the children must get out,' he ordered. 'Go and collect buffalo droppings and make a fire. Louise has to boil as much water as she can.'

Before Louise left the wagon, she filled the big kettle with water, scooping it up in a little tin bowl from the barrel in the back of the wagon. She cast a timid glance at her mother, who lay still and white on the tarpaulin. Mother caught Louise's eye and gave her a gentle, encouraging nod. If only that doctor would come quickly!

The doctor came.

With his long legs, he stepped from the saddle into the wagon in one stride. John tied up his horse. Then he wiped the sweat and dust out of his eyes with the back of his hand.

To the children, it seemed to take a long time. The water had already been boiling for quite a while. No one had asked for it yet, and they did not dare to look into the wagon.

In the distance ahead of them hung a thick cloud of dust, behind which the caravan was hidden. They would fall very far to the rear. John looked worried. He knew that that was danger-ous – stragglers ran the risk of being attacked; but he said nothing. Now and again his father came out and glanced around, scanned the trail behind them – eight sets of wagon wheels beside each other and thousands upon thousands of hoof marks. But behind, the horizon was clear and empty.

Until John suddenly perceived a tiny cloud of dust.

He started. He knew that that could only mean one thing.

'Father!' he shouted.

Henry Sager stuck his head out of the wagon.

John pointed to the east, where the cloud of dust above their own tracks had now grown rather larger.

Father Sager said nothing.

He went back into the wagon with the kettle of boiling water, but came out again a moment later with five rifles and two pistols. John had already pulled his own pistol from its holster. His father gave him a rifle.

'All the children except John and Louise, get under the wagon,' he commanded quietly. But it was easy to see that that calmness of his required all the self-control he had. His strong, wrinkled neck was fiery red, and the veins on his forehead were thick and purple.

'Take these,' he said to his eldest daughter, and Lousie stood with three rifles in her arms, staring at the approaching cloud of dust as if turned to stone.

Father put the powder horn, lead, and ramrods down beside her.

John had laid his rifle across the saddlebow in front of him, as he had always seen the trappers do.

But his father said:

'Are you mad, boy? Get down and tie the horse up in front, along with the oxen. Do you want to serve as a target, and be shot out of the saddle?'

Francis pushed the smaller children under the wagon. Catherine began to resist, crying and kicking. 'Stop howling, you little idiot,' Francis snapped nervously, trying to make his voice sound as manly as possible. Matilda and Lizzy thought it rather a nice game; as a rule, they were never allowed to go under the wagon.

Father Sager climbed back in again.

He brought out two empty water casks, and the only bag of flour they had left. He stood the two casks upright beside the wagon, near one of the rear wheels, and laid the sack of flour across them.

'Come to the back here,' he ordered John and Louise.

'And remember – don't stir from cover. We fire along to one side of this, and between the casks. … Louise, you load the rifles when we've fired them,' he said to her. To John he said nothing; he only looked at him.

A sound came from the wagon. It was like the crying of a tiny baby.

Father Sager gritted his teeth, and behaved as if he had not heard anything. The sound came again, more distinctly this time. Then he looked at his two eldest children; he almost had tears in his eyes.

'May God help us to protect that young life,' he said between clenched teeth. Rather more calmly, he went on: 'If it comes to that, it's not certain that they mean mischief. And our rifles are good, sound ones. John, don't fire too soon, let 'em get close.'

He put his head back into the wagon.

'Don't worry, Doctor – we'll call if we can't manage without you.'

They waited in suspense. It was now easy to see that the cause of the cloud was horsemen – not many, perhaps half a dozen, on prairie ponies. They were superior in numbers, but they could not take cover anywhere.

There was no brushwood in which they could ensconce themselves.

'May God help us to protect that young life,' Father had said.

Those words made an indelible impression on John.

There, inside the wagon, a new brother or sister was lying – they did not even know yet which it was; but it was a new life, and it was theirs. It had been given to them to take care of. Mother had had so much trouble to bring it into the world, and now Father and he had to see to it that … just imagine, suppose something should happen to it!

John got even hotter than he was already. He pushed his hat to the back of his head, and wiped his dusty, sweaty face with his sleeve for the umpteenth time. He spat on the ground.

During the ride up to the front of the caravan to fetch the doctor, he had felt as if he was biting the dust that had been stirred up. If only it would rain! Queer, that … that he should think of rain at this moment.

The horsemen were so close now that he could see that one of them was carrying a rifle; the others had bows and arrows.

There … the first arrow came whizzing through the air. Its iron tip bored through the canvas cover of the wagon; the feathered tail stood buzzing and quivering.

A shot rang out, but Father motioned to John to hold his hand.

Then … they both fired at the same time.

The foremost rider, the one with the rifle, fell sideways from his horse, wounded. The animal dragged him a short distance along the ground. The other members of the troop swerved away immediately, rode round in a great circle at tremendous speed, and charged again.

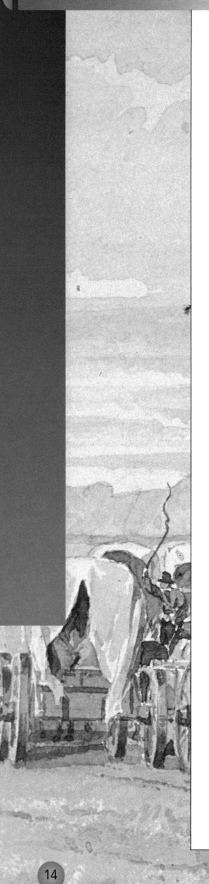

Once more Henry and John Sager fired their two rifles, while the arrows whistled above their heads.

Number two was shot out of the saddle. One of his comrades seized him just in time, and pulled him on to his horse, in front of him.

John's hat was whipped from his head, a dry tap sounded; he glanced round. An arrow had drilled its way deep into the woodwork of the wagon, carrying hat and all. Then he heard a splash – he just glimpsed the arms of the doctor, who had emptied a bowl of water out through the tilt.

Louise pushed another freshly loaded rifle into his hands. But it was no longer necessary. The horsemen had now picked up the first of their two wounded, and were galloping off in a wide arc. The two riderless ponies were running far away in the distance. Soon there was nothing to be seen but slowly settling dust.

'Cattle thieves,' said father Sager brusquely. 'They'll have been disappointed.'

He took the sack of flour and climbed into the wagon with it. An arrow had pierced it; a white trail of its precious contents was trickling down through a little hole.

A moment later he stuck his head outside again:

'You can all come in,' he said solemnly.

One by one they climbed into the wagon, John leading the way. He tried to behave very sedately, but inwardly he was trembling. Louise had John's hat in her hands, and was trying to smooth out the dents in it. Cathie gave Francis a push, so that he nearly fell on his face as he climbed in; that was her way of revenging herself for just now. Stretching out his long arms in their striped flannel shirt sleeves, Henry Sager lifted Matilda and Lizzy from the ground.

The red of all those children's shirts, so bright in the sun outside, became dark in the darkness of the wagon. And there lay Mother, like a beautiful picture in black and white, her pale face with those much too big eyes laughing sweetly up at them, and her long dark hair spread out on both sides of her head against the white canvas. The doctor threw away a last bowl of water, dried his hands, and gave Father Sager a hearty slap on the back. Only then did the children see that Father was holding something in his arms. It was a baby, washed and combed, with a big forelock of black hair, but for the rest looking ridiculously tiny in Mother's purple silk shawl.

'She'll weigh about nine pounds, I guess – an *enormous* child!' said the doctor.

John glanced at Louise; but Louise was gazing fascinated at the baby. Then he looked at Francis, who looked back at him with a grin. An enormous child! It was really laughable. But the baby was a girl – that was nice. A new little sister, a very small sister … perhaps it was because they had just escaped from great danger, while the baby was being born, or because, after that fight, John felt more of a man than ever; but, in any case, he had a burning desire to take his little sister in his arms, and protect her against everything for always.

But Father put the baby down again beside its mother.

They went on their knees in a circle round mother and child. The doctor and Father took their hats off; John tore his from Louise's hands, and held the damaged hat over his chest, with folded hands, just like Father, and closed his eyes. His father prayed aloud in a firm, deep voice:

'O Lord, we commend this child to Your care. Her name shall be Indepentia, which means independence. And she shall be baptized in the new land, in the valley of the River Columbia in Oregon, Amen.'

Reading for meaning

1   a)   Why does the writer describe the packing up and setting off of the caravan in so much detail?

   b)   Why were there so many rules for the wagon drivers?

2   What makes you realise that Mr Sager depends on John more than on his other children?

3   How does the writer make the younger Sager children seem real?

4   Is Mr Sager calm throughout this episode? How do you know?

5   What makes you interested in what is going to happen next?

Vocabulary and spelling

1   *Children on the Oregon Trail* was first published in 1954, but it is set over one hundred years earlier, in 1844. Skim the text again: find clues which suggest that it takes place in the past. Look for details of:

-   the setting

-   what the characters say and do

-   whose point of view the story puts over most strongly.

2   a)   Look for all the different **verbs** used where the writer *could have used* 'said'. Why has he chosen these verbs? What effect do they create?

   b)   Look for all the places where the writer *has used* the verb 'said'. Suggest a different verb that could be used in each case. What difference does it make to the meaning of the text?

3   The following words appear in the second paragraph of this text: guards, women, families, children.

   a)   What rules for forming plurals do these words illustrate?

   b)   Write the rules and some examples in your spelling log.

4   In the text, it says that 'It was hot and stuffy under the canvas tilts, which were thick with dust'. Look up the word 'tilts' in your dictionary: does it help? Probably not!

So, what do you think 'tilts' could mean? How can you try to work it out? How might you check your reasoning?

A **verb** is a word which describes what a person or thing *does* or *is*, for example *The man **walks**, The door **is** over there.* Verbs are often described as 'doing' or 'being' words.

Well-chosen verbs help writers to convey character or action effectively. In this text, for example, Mr Sager 'ordered' and 'commanded' and Francis 'snapped', which are much more interesting verbs to use than 'said', as they give us information about the characters – that Mr Sager always expected to be obeyed, and that Francis was feeling tense at that moment.

Sentences, paragraphs and punctuation

1   The opening paragraph of this text consists of just one short sentence.

    a) Look for other short paragraphs in the text.
    b) What different effects does this technique have?

2   In the second paragraph, the writer uses the **passive voice** in the sentence 'Bacon was fried, coffee was made, by those who still had some.'

    a) How would this sentence be written in the active voice?
    b) Why do you think the passive voice was used at this point?

3   a) Explain why the **semi-colon** is the correct punctuation to use in this sentence: 'The doctor was a veterinary surgeon; the emigrants did not have a real doctor with them.'

    b) Could the sentence have been punctuated differently?

4   Look again at the first part of the text, from 'That day began like any other' to 'A new, hard day had begun.'

    How does the writer help you understand the order in which things happen and how long everything takes to get ready?

The **active** and **passive voices** in verbs affect the meaning of a text.
* The active voice puts the doer of an action early in the sentence: for example, 'Francis pushed the smaller children under the wagon.'
* If the passive voice is used, the sentence is turned round so that the doer comes at the end: 'The small children were pushed under the wagon by Francis.' The effect is less dramatic and less immediate.

Writing to persuade, argue and advise

We don't know why the Sagers set off on their journey. Think of some possible reasons.

Imagine you are either Mr or Mrs Sager. Write a letter to a friend you have left behind. You are writing on the day after the birth of Indepentia.

In the letter:

● argue that you were right to leave your home

● try to *persuade* your friend that their family should follow you

● tell them about some of the difficulties they might face, and advise them how to overcome them.

Think about:

● the news and information you would include

● how honest you would be about your experiences so far

● the sort of language you would use

● what you want your friend to feel on reading the letter.

Make sure that your letter presents a strong case which is likely to succeed in persuading your friend. For example, you could:

● refer to your friends's interests, and how the journey would be enjoyable

● emphasise key points by repeating them

● exaggerate the good experiences you have had, and underplay the difficulties

● involve your friend by using **rhetorical questions**.

Rhetorical questions are questions in a text which *either*:
• do not require an answer, or
• you cannot answer.
They are a useful for making you feel as if the writer is speaking directly to you, and for making you think about important issues or ideas. After all, if a writer asks you a question, it's very hard to ignore, isn't it? (Of course, that last sentence was an example of a rhetorical question!)

New Baby

Now read the poem by Jackie Kay on page 20. The point of view is that of a child whose way of life has suddenly changed.

Before you read

1 How might an older child feel when a new baby arrives?

- Does it matter how old he or she is?

- Does it matter if the older child is a boy or girl?

- Does the sex of the baby make any difference?

2 How could a writer try to make a text sound like a child's view of a situation? *Hint: Think about the subject matter, choice of words, and* **rhyme** *and* **rhythm** *in a poem.*

Rhythm is the pattern of long and short, or strong and weak, beats in a text. The word 'pattern', for example, consists of a long/strong syllable followed by a short/weak syllable.

Rhyme may be regular or irregular. Regular rhyme can be used to make a poem easy to remember, or it may be used for particular effects, for example, to link words which are important to the meaning of a text. Some poems use half-rhyme, for example 'noise' and 'mice' in Jackie Kay's poem, which sounds like a 'wrong note' in music. So it can be useful to make you think about the words or to suggest a sense of unhappiness.

Reading for meaning

When you have read the poem, answer these questions.

1 Think about all the real and imaginary things the child mentions in this poem. Why do you think the poet has included them?

2 What do you think the last line of the poem means? *Hint: Do the speaker's feelings change?*

3 Does this poem have a serious subject? *Hint: Think about that last line.*

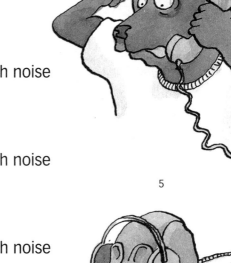

New Baby

My baby brother makes so much noise
that the Rottweiler next door
phoned up to complain.

My baby brother makes so much noise
that all the big green frogs   5
came out the drains.

My baby brother makes so much noise
that the rats and the mice
wore headphones.

My baby brother makes so much noise   10
that I can't ask my mum a question,
so much noise that sometimes

I think of sitting the cat on top of him
in his pretty little cot with all his teddies.
But even the cat is terrified of his cries.   15

So I have devised a plan. A soundproof room.
A telephone to talk to my mum.
A small lift to receive food and toys.

Thing is, it will cost a fortune.
The other thing is, the frogs have gone.   20
It's not bad now. Not that I like him or anything.

In the Nursery

This poem by Anne Stevenson describes another young baby. It is very different from 'New Baby', both in how it is written (its style) and in what it says (its content). It is also written from a different point of view: the mother's, not a brother's or a sister's.

As you read

Think about:

● what the poet compares the baby to

● what *she* feels about her baby

● how the poem makes *you* feel about the mother and child.

In the Nursery

I lift the seven months baby from his crib,
a clump of roots.
Sleep drops off him like soil
in clods that smell sunbaked and rich with urine.
He opens his eyes,
two light blue corollas.
His cheek against mine
is the first soft day in the garden.
His mouth makes a bud, then a petal,
then a leaf.
In less than seven seconds
he's blossoming in a bowl of arms.

Simile is when the writer creates a picture in your mind by *comparing* one thing to something else, using the words 'as' or 'like' to link the objects. For example, in this poem, 'sleep drops off him *like* soil in clods'.

Metaphor is when the author writes about something as if it is something else so you see it in a new or different way. For example, in this poem, Anne Stevenson does not just *compare* the baby to a growing plant, she writes about him as if he actually *is* a plant ('a clump of roots') being lifted from his cradle.

Reading for meaning

1 Anne Stevenson compares her son to a flowering plant. Do you think this comparison works well? For example:

- Do you expect a baby to be compared to a plant? What does it make you think about?

- How do the difficult or unusual words add to the effect of the poem?

- What differences are there between the last two lines and the first four lines?

2 What do you think the poet feels about the baby? Pick out some words or phrases which support your idea.

Language variation

The two poems you have just read are different in lots of ways. One of these differences is the kind of language used by each poet.

- The language in 'New Baby' is **informal**, and is intended to sound like a child speaking.

- The language of 'In the Nursery' is more **formal**, and is intended to sound like the thoughts of a mother.

With a partner, look for examples of language (for example, vocabulary, patterns such as repetition, grammatical constructions such as complete or incomplete sentences) which illustrate:

- the speech-like and child-like nature of 'New Baby'

- the formal, adult nature of 'In the Nursery'

- any similarities in the language or grammar of the two poems.

Formal language follows the conventions of **standard English.** You would use it to write to someone in authority, for example.
Informal language:
- can follow the grammatical conventions of standard English but include **contractions**, such as 'wouldn't' or 'can't', for example if you are speaking to an elderly relative, or
- can be non-standard English, for example if you use **slang** with a friend.

Standard English is the accepted language of public communication, which follows commonly-accepted rules or conventions of vocabulary choice, spelling, punctuation and grammar. It does not use **slang**, outdated or regional forms of language. Examples of non-standard English include **verb** forms such as 'we was' instead of 'we were' or 'him and me was ...' instead of 'he and I were ...'.

Writing to analyse, review and comment

1 Find out which of the two poems, 'New Baby' and 'In the Nursery', most people in your class prefer, and why. Work out a way of presenting your findings in a table, using columns and headings.

2 Write a paragraph summarising their views, and a second paragraph explaining your own view and commenting on other people's views.

Writing to imagine, explore and entertain

Imagine that these two poems are about the same baby – the *speaker* of 'In the Nursery' is actually the *mum* mentioned in 'New Baby'!

Write a conversation the mother and elder child have several years later. They compare their memories and feelings about the new baby. Write the conversation as a playscript. If you can, look at a printed playscript to see how names, stage directions and so on are set out.

Speaking and listening

In a small group, prepare a reading of these two poems. In your planning and preparation, think about whether:

- to use one or more separate readers for each poem
- choral speaking or separate voices would be better
- the poems need different types of voices or not.

Try to think of any other important planning points before you perform your reading to the rest of the class. For example, will you include actions, facial expressions or sound effects?

Reading for meaning

1 How does the shape or form of 'New Baby' help to convey its meaning to you? For example:

- Why do the first four stanzas (verses) all start with the same line?
- Why is there no full stop at the end of the fourth stanza?
- What is the effect of the word 'So' at the start of the sixth stanza?
- Why is the last stanza made up of four short sentences?

2 What two meanings could the title 'In the Nursery' have? Why are both meanings appropriate to the poem?

3 How important are rhyme, rhythm and **sounds** in 'New Baby' and 'In the Nursery'?

Sounds in poetry may include:
- **assonance** – repeated vowel sounds, for example 'came out the drains'
- **alliteration** – when connected syllables or words begin with the same letter or sound, for example 'baby brother'
- **onomatopoeia** – the use of words which sound like their meaning, for example 'cries'.

The Growing Pains of Adrian Mole

The final text in this section is a selection of diary extracts written by a fictional teenager, Adrian Mole. The first diary entry describes a dreadful discovery he has made. The other entries cover significant events which take place over the following year.

As you read

Think about:

- how you would describe Adrian's personality

- what sort of relationship he has with the adults he mentions in his diary

- what he really feels about his new sister, Rosie.

Reading for meaning

When you have read the text, answer these questions.

1   What are Adrian's reasons for being upset at his mother's news?

2   How do you know that Adrian does not understand much about babies?

3   Which of Adrian's diary entries suggest that:

    a)   he likes having a baby sister?

    b)   he is jealous of her?

4   What do you learn about Adrian from the diary entry for Thursday September 2nd?

5   What different kinds of humour are there in the entry for the day when Rosie is born? *Hint: Think about the situation, what people do and what they say.*

6   Sue Townsend, who wrote this book, is an adult woman pretending to be a teenage boy. How does this affect your view of Adrian? *Hint: Think about how the writer chooses what to describe and how to describe it. How might she have made Adrian seem very different?*

THE GROWING PAINS OF ADRIAN MOLE

Wednesday May 26th

My mother is pregnant! My mother!!!!!!!!!

I will be the laughing stock at school. How could she do this to me? She is three months pregnant already, so in November a baby will be living in this house. I hope they don't expect me to share my room with it. There's no way I'm getting up in the night to give it a bottle.

My parents didn't prepare me or anything. We were all eating spaghetti on toast when my father said casually, 'Oh, by the way, Adrian, congratulations are in order, your mother's three months pregnant.'

Congratulations! What about my 'A' levels in two years' time? How can I study with a toddler smashing the place up around me?

10 p.m. Kissed my poor mother goodnight. She said, 'Are you pleased about the baby, Adrian?' I lied and said 'Yes.' …

Friday June 18th

I pretended to be enthusiastic about the baby at breakfast today. I asked my mother if she had thought of any names yet. My mother said, 'Yes, I'm going to call her Christabel.'

Christabel! It sounds like somebody out of *Peter Pan*. Nobody is called Christabel. The poor kid. …

Wednesday June 30th

My mother wants to move. She wants to sell the house that I have lived in all my life. She said that we will need more room 'for the baby.' How stupid can you get? Babies hardly take any space at all. They are only about twenty-one inches long. …

Thursday September 2nd

There is now no disguising the fact that my mother is pregnant. She sticks right out at the front and walks in a very peculiar manner. She finds it a bit difficult to bend down, so I spend half my time picking things up for her.

Her dungarees are too tight for her, so I am hoping that she will buy a pretty flowery maternity dress. Princess Diana looked charming during her pregnancy. One of those big white collars would really suit my mother. Also it would distract attention from her wrinkly neck. …

Tuesday September 7th

Went to the ante-natal clinic with my mother. We waited for two hours in a room full of red-faced pregnant women. My mother had forgotten to bring a sample of urine from home, so a nurse gave her a shiny oven tray and told her to, 'Squeeze a few drops out for us, dear.'

My mother had only just been to the loo so she took ages and ended up missing her place in the weighing queue. By the time her blood pressure was taken my mother was in a state of hypertension. She said the doctor warned her about doing too much and told her to relax more. …

Tuesday October 19th

Mrs Singh accompanied my mother to the ante-natal clinic today. The gynaecologist has told my mother she must rest more or she will be forced into hospital and made to stay in bed. Her swollen ankles are caused by high blood pressure. She is dead old to be having a baby so the doctors are giving her more attention in case she dies and they get into trouble. …

Thursday November 11th
ARMISTICE DAY

When I got home from school my mother's little suitcase was missing from the hall. She was nowhere in the house, but I found a note on the biscuit tin. It said:

> Waters broke at 3.35. I am in the labour ward of the Royal Infirmary. Call a taxi. £5 note at bottom of spaghetti jar. Don't worry.
>   Love, Mum
> P.S. Dog at Mrs Singh's.

Her writing looked dead untidy.

The taxi ride was a nightmare. I was struggling to get my hand free of the spaghetti jar all the way. The taxi driver kept saying. 'You should have tipped the jar upside down, you stupid beggar.'

He parked outside the entrance to the hospital, and watched the jar versus my hand struggle in a bored sort of way. He said, 'I'll have to charge you waiting time.' A hundred years passed: then he said, 'And I can't change a five-pound note either.'

I was almost in tears by the time I managed to pull my

hand out. I had a mental image of my mother calling for me. So I gave the taxi driver the fiver, and ran into the hospital. Found the lift and pressed the button which said 'Labour Ward.'

I emerged into another world. It looked like the space control centre at Houston.

A technician asked, 'Who are you?'

I said, 'I'm Adrian Mole.'

And you've got permission to visit the labour ward?'

'Yes,' I said. (Why did I say yes? Why?)

'Room 13. She's being a bit stubborn.'

'Yes, she's a stubborn kind of person.' I said, and walked down the corridor. Doors opened and shut and I caught glimpses of women hooked up to gruesome-looking equipment. Moans and groans bounced around the shiny floors. I pushed the door of Room 13 open and saw my mother lying on a high bed reading *Memoirs of a Fox-hunting Man* by Siegfried Sassoon.

She looked pleased to see me and then asked why I'd brought the spaghetti jar into the hospital. I was halfway through telling her, when she screwed her face up and started singing 'Hard Day's Night'.

After a bit she stopped singing and looked normal. She even laughed when I got to the bit about the horrible taxi driver. After a bit a kind black nurse came in and said, 'Are you all right, honey?'

My mother said, 'Yes. This is Adrian.'

The nurse said, 'Put a mask and gown on, Adrian, and sit in a corner; it's going to be action stations soon!'

After about half an hour my mother was singing more and talking less. She kept grabbing my hand and crushing it. The nurse came back in and to my relief told me to go out. But my mother wouldn't let go of my hand. The nurse told me to make myself useful and time the contractions. When she'd gone I asked my mother what contractions were.

'Pains,' she said, between clenched teeth. I asked her why she hadn't had her back frozen to stop the pain. My mother said, 'I can't stand people fiddling around with my back.'

The pains started coming every minute, and my mother went barmy, and a lot of people ran in and started telling her to push. I sat in a far corner at the head end of my mother and tried not to look at the other end where doctors and nurses were clanging about with metal things. My mother was puffing and panting, just like she does at Christmas when she's blowing balloons up. Soon everyone was shouting. 'Push, Mrs Mole, push!' My mother pushed until her eyes nearly popped out. 'Harder,' they shouted. My mother went a bit barmy again, and the doctor said, 'I can see the baby's head!'

I tried to escape then but my mother said, 'Where's Adrian? I want Adrian.'

I didn't like to leave her alone with strangers, so I said I'd stay. I stared at the beauty spot on my mother's cheek for the next three minutes, and I didn't look up, until I heard the black nurse say, 'Pant for the head.'

At 5.19 p.m. my mother had a barmy moment; then the doctor and nurses gave a sort of loud sigh, and I looked up and saw a skinny purple thing hanging upside down. It was covered in white stuff.

'It's a lovely little girl, Mrs Mole,' the doctor said, and he looked dead pleased, as if he were the father himself.

My mother said, 'Is she all right?'

The doctor said, 'Toes and fingers all correct.'

The baby started crying in a crotchety, bad-tempered way, and she was put on my mother's flatter belly. My mother looked at her as if she was a precious piece of jewellery or something. I congratulated my mother and she said, 'Say hello to your sister.'

The doctor stared at me in my mask and gown and said, 'Aren't you Mr Mole, the baby's father?'

I said, 'No, I'm Master Mole the baby's brother.'

'Then you've broken every rule in this hospital,' he said. 'I must ask you to leave. You could be rife with childish infectious diseases.'

So, while they stood around waiting for something called the placenta to emerge, I went into the corridor. I found a waiting-room full of worried-looking men, smoking and talking about cars.

Then went home. I walked around the empty house, trying to imagine sharing it with a little girl.

I put all my smashable possessions on the top shelf of my unit. Then went to bed. It was only 7.30 but for some reason I was dead tired. The phone woke me up at 8.15. It was my father gibbering about having a girl. He wanted to know every detail about her. I said she took after him. Half bald and angry-looking. …

Monday November 22nd

We had to write a description of a person in English. So I wrote about Rosie.

Rosie

Rosie is about eighteen inches long, she has got a big head with fuzzy black hair in a Friar Tuck style. Unlike the rest of our family, her eyes are brown. She has got quite a good skin. Her mouth is extremely small, except when she is screaming. Then it resembles an underground cavern. She has got a wrinkled-up neck like a turkey's. She dresses in unisex clothes, and always wears disposable nappies. She lazes about all day in a carrycot and only gets out when it is time to be fed or changed. She has got a split personality; calm one minute, screaming like a maniac the next.

She is only eleven days old but she rules our house. ...

Saturday November 27th

Changed my first nappy tonight.

Tomorrow I am going to try doing it with my eyes open.

Sunday November 28th

How is it that my mother can change Rosie's yukky nappies and at the same time smile and even laugh? I nearly fainted when I tried to do it without a protective device (clothes peg). Perhaps women have got poorly developed nasal passages. ...

Monday February 28th

Rosie has got her first tooth. My index finger is still bleeding. ...

Monday March 21st

My parents have hardly spoken to me since Friday night. They are too busy watching Rosie's manual dexterity develop.

Every time the kid grabs a plastic brick or shoves a rusk in her mouth, she gets a round of applause. ...

Sunday May 22nd

Rosie started crawling at 5 p.m.

My parents gave her a standing ovation.

Vocabulary and spelling

Adrian sometimes uses the correct technical language when he is writing about childbirth, for example 'ante-natal', 'gynaecologist', 'placenta'.

1   What do these terms mean? Why do you think Adrian uses them?

2   In small groups, carry out the following investigation and prepare three posters to show your findings in each case.

   a)   What does the prefix 'ante-' mean? Find some other words in which it is used and make sure that you know what they mean.

   b)   What does the suffix '-ologist' mean? Find some other words in which it is used and make sure you know what they mean.

   c)   Find some other words in the same family as 'placenta' and think about how their meanings are connected. You will need to look up 'placenta' in a dictionary and follow any leads from there! *Hint: An* **etymological** *dictionary may be helpful.*

Etymology is the study of the origin and history of words:
• the language(s) they come from
• how their meanings may have changed over time
• other words which are related to them.
An **etymological** dictionary traces these origins of words.

Language variation

1   With a partner, find places where Adrian uses a mixture of formal, **standard English** and **slang**.

2   Why do you think he does this? What is the effect it achieves?

3   Prepare some notes to use in a class discussion about the language used in this text. Use the following headings to organise your notes:

   ● Examples of formal, standard English

   ● Examples of informal language or slang

   ● How different words help us to understand Adrian's character

   ● How different words create humour and make us laugh.

Punctuation

1   The exclamation mark is used differently in the first two diary entries. What different effects does this have?

2   Look again at the description of Rosie written by Adrian in his English lesson on Monday November 22nd.

   a) Is the punctuation he uses always correct?
   b) Are there alternatives, and would they affect the meaning?

Writing to inform, explain and describe

Think about a person who has been an important influence in your life, or who has made a big impression on you. This should be somebody you know, not a famous person you admire.

Write a detailed description of this person which:

- provides accurate and truthful *information* of their appearance

- *describes* what he or she is like

- *explains* why he or she is so important to you.

Use examples of the kinds of things the person says or does to make your description lively and interesting.

Use the planning sheet to help you organise your ideas before you begin to write.

1.2 Autobiography

Every family is a unique mixture of personalities, with different interests, ambitions and worries. The texts in this section explore three families and the relationships between the parents and the children.

An **autobiography** is the story of someone's life written by himself or herself, usually in the **first person**. You need to read autobiographies with care – the writer may leave out events which show him or her in a bad light, and may exaggerate, or even invent, other episodes which make him or her look good. Which of the three autobiographies in this section do you think is the most trustworthy, and why?

A **biography** is the story of someone's life written by somebody else, usually in the **third person**. You need to read biographies with care as they will always contain a number of opinions – the author's and maybe other people's too.

My Early Life

The first text is an extract from *My Early Life*, the **autobiography** of the famous politician and writer, Winston Churchill.

By the time that Winston was seven, his parents had decided that he was 'a troublesome boy' who should no longer be taught at home by a governess. So, he was sent to a boarding school to prepare him for Eton, a public school attended by the sons of many rich families, including some of the present royal family. His first experience of formal education was not very promising, as you will see.

Before you read

1 Why do you think someone would choose to write their autobiography? Whose autobiographies would a publisher be interested in publishing, do you think?

2 How do you think writers choose what to include in an autobiography?

3 Can a person remember in detail things that happened a long time ago?

MY EARLY LIFE

The fateful day arrived. My mother took me to the station in a hansom cab. She gave me three half-crowns which I dropped on to the floor of the cab, and we had to scramble about in the straw to find them again. We only just caught the train. If we had missed it, it would have been the end of the world. However, we didn't, and the world went on.

The school my parents had selected for my education was one of the most fashionable and expensive in the country. It modelled itself upon Eton and aimed at being preparatory for that Public School above all others. It was supposed to be the very last thing in schools. Only ten boys in a class; electric light (then a wonder); a swimming pond; spacious football and cricket grounds; two or three school treats, or 'expeditions' as they were called, every term; the masters all M.A.'s in gowns and mortar-boards; a chapel of its own; no hampers allowed; everything provided by the authority. It was a dark November afternoon when we arrived at the establishment. We had tea with the Headmaster, with whom my mother conversed in the most easy manner. I was preoccupied with the fear of spilling my cup and so making 'a bad start.' I was also miserable at the idea of being left alone among all these strangers in this great, fierce, formidable place. After all I was only seven, and I had been so happy in my nursery with all my toys. I had such wonderful toys: a real steam engine, a magic lantern, and a collection of soldiers already nearly a thousand strong. Now it was to be all lessons.

Seven or eight hours of lessons every day except half-holidays, and football or cricket in addition.

When the last sound of my mother's departing wheels had died away, the Headmaster invited me to hand over any money I had in my possession. I produced my three half-crowns which were duly entered in a book, and I was told that from time to time there would be a 'shop' at the school with all sorts of things which one would like have, and that I could choose what I liked up to the limit of the seven and sixpence. Then we quitted the Headmaster's parlour and the comfort-able private side of the house, and entered the more bleak apartments reserved for the instruction and accommodation of the pupils. I was taken into a Form Room and told to sit at a desk. All the other boys were out of doors, and I was alone with the Form Master. He produced a thin greeny-brown-covered book filled with words in different types of print.

'You have never done any Latin before, have you?' he said.

'No, sir.'

'This is a Latin grammar.' He opened it at a well-thumbed page. 'You must learn this,' he said, pointing to a number of words in a frame of lines. 'I will come back in half an hour and see what you know.'

Behold me then on a gloomy evening, with an aching heart, seated in front of the First Declension.

Mensa	a table
Mensa	O table
Mensam	a table
Mensae	of a table
Mensae	to or for a table
Mensa	by, with or from a table

What on earth did it mean? Where was the sense of it? It seemed absolute rigmarole to me. However, there was one thing I could always do: I could learn by heart. And I thereupon proceeded, as far as my private sorrows would allow, to memorise the task which had been set me.

In due course the Master returned.

'Have you learnt it?' he asked.

'I think I can *say* it, sir,' I replied; and I gabbled it off.

He seemed so satisfied with this that I was emboldened to ask a question.

'What does it mean, sir?'

'It means what it says. Mensa, a table. Mensa is a noun of the First Declension. There are five declensions. You have learnt the singular of the First Declension.'

'But,' I repeated, 'what does it mean?'

'Mensa means table,' he answered.

'Then why does mensa also mean O table,' I enquired, 'and what does O table mean?'

'Mensa, O table, is the vocative case,' he replied.

'But why O table?' I persisted in genuine curiosity.

'O table, – you would use that in addressing a table, in invoking a table.' And then seeing he was not carrying me with him, 'You would use it in speaking to a table.'

'But I never do,' I blurted out in honest amazement.

'If you are impertinent, you will be punished, and punished, let me tell you, very severely,' was his conclusive rejoinder.

Such was my first introduction to the classics from which, I have been told, many of our cleverest men have derived so much solace and profit.

Latin was the language of Ancient Rome. Because the Roman Empire extended so widely throughout the ancient world, Latin has influenced many modern languages. When it was no longer used as a daily language, it remained in use for religious and legal ceremonies. Latin was widely taught as a school subject until the 1960s. It is still taught in most public schools and in a few state schools.

Reading for meaning

1   How you know that the events described in this text took place some time in the past? *Hint: Think about things that are mentioned and the way people speak and behave to each other.*

2   What are your impressions of the school that Winston has been sent to? Do they change as you read the text? *Hint: Think about what he knows before he goes there and what it actually seems like.*

3   How does the third paragraph show that Winston is feeling more and more miserable about the place he has been left in?

4   What impression does the Form Master get of Winston? What does this tell you about the Form Master's attitude towards young children?

5   What is the meaning of the last paragraph?

Vocabulary and spelling

Work with a partner on these tasks.

1   What effect does Churchill create in the phrase 'this great, fierce, formidable' place?

2   Churchill writes 'I was emboldened to ask a question.' To 'embolden' is a verb made from the adjective 'bold'. What verbs which are made from the following adjectives:
a) strong?
b) beautiful?
c) sad?
d) lazy?
e) short?

3   Churchill uses a number of words and phrases which qualify or compare the objects they describe, for example 'one of the most and absolute'. Find other words and phrases of this kind, and make sure that you understand what they mean.

4   The following words from the text illustrate four different ways of spelling the same vowel sound: 'fateful', 'day', 'train', 'great'.
a) Think of another word which illustrates each different spelling.
b) Think of other words which illustrate yet more ways of spelling the same sound.

5 The **participle** 'aching' in the text derives from the **verb** 'ache'.
  a) What spelling rule does this illustrate?
  b) Think of three other verbs to illustrate the same rule.

> The present **participle** is a verb form which shows a continuous action; it ends in '-ing' and, although it is called 'present', it can be used with any tense, for example 'she *is walking*', 'she *was walking*', 'she *will be walking*'. It can be used as an adjective, for example 'the *laughing* man'.

Sentences and paragraphs

1 'We had tea with the Headmaster, with whom my mother conversed in the most easy manner.'
  a) Suggest how this information could be structured into one or more sentences. Think of several different ways.
  b) Which is the best, and why?

2 Look at the structure of the second paragraph.
  a) What is the topic sentence?
  b) How does the whole paragraph add to the topic sentence?

Language variation

This text was written in about 1930, and some of the language may seem quite **formal** or old-fashioned to you.
a) Look for some words, phrases or constructions which are unfamiliar or unusual. What do they mean?
b) Why has Churchill has used them? *Hint: Think about* **irony**, *the time in which the text is set, and when it was written.*

> **Irony** is a kind of humour based on mockery or gentle sarcasm. If you say, 'He's a very nice man', but mean the opposite, that is irony. When Winston is made to feel that 'it would have been the end of the world' to miss the train and then comments 'However, we didn't, and the world went on', he is being ironic because he is mocking his mother's over-dramatic reactions.

Punctuation

1   In this text, apostrophes are used in several different ways. Explain why an apostrophe is used in each of the following examples:
    a) didn't
    b) M.A.'s
    c) mother's.

2   In the second paragraph, the long fourth sentence is punctuated with a number of **semi-colons**. Explain why this is appropriate here.

3   Explain the use of the **colon** in this sentence from the second paragraph: 'I had such wonderful toys: a real steam engine, a magic lantern, and a collection of soldiers already nearly a thousand strong.'

The **semi-colon** is a punctuation mark which has two main uses.

• It can separate phrases or clauses in a sentence when you want a clearer break than a comma, but not a full stop. For example, in the sentence 'Mushtaq supports Arsenal; I am a fan of Chelsea.' the two statements are connected, and so do not need to be split by a full stop. The semi-colon indicates more clearly than a comma that there is a contrast between the two parts of the sentence.

• It can separate items in a list, for example, in the second paragraph of this text. Commas could also be used here, but the semi-colon suggests a more significant break. Churchill uses it to impress on you the full wonder of each aspect of the school.

The most common use of the **colon** is to introduce a list. It is also used to introduce a quotation or to introduce a second clause in a sentence which adds to the first, for example 'He felt very ill: he really should not have eaten the third cream cake.'

Writing to persuade, argue and advise

You have been asked to speak in a class debate on the advantages and disadvantages of boarding schools. Write your opening statement in which you try to persuade your listeners that boarding schools are either a good idea or a bad idea. Remember to plan your speech carefully, so that you:

● include appropriate information and opinions

● catch your listeners' interest at the start, and keep it to the end

● use **persuasive** language and techniques.

To **persuade** an audience, remember to use some of the following:
• **facts** which support your case
• **opinions** presented as facts, for example 'Everybody knows that …'
• personal experiences or **anecdotes**
• dramatic, exaggerated or biased language
• **rhetorical questions**, for example 'What do you think is the point of that?'
• rhythmical and grammatical sequences, for example 'He was a cheat, a liar, a rogue; first he said one thing, then he said another'.

Drama

Prepare and perform one of the following activities.

1 Plan and rehearse the conversation between Winston and his mother when he dropped his money in the cab. The first paragraph suggests it was a lively conversation!

Remember to:

● look in the text for hints about what might have been said

● think about the feelings Winston and his mother might have had.

● use the kind of language you think they would have spoken.

2 Imagine that the Headmaster has asked the Form Master what he thinks of his new pupil after their first meeting. Improvise their conversation, making sure that you:

● include details of what has actually happened

● add the comments you think both men might make

● use the kind of language you think they would have spoken.

Papa and Mama

The next text is the opening chapter of Roald Dahl's **autobiography**, *Boy*. In it, he describes how his father became a wealthy businessman and recounts some events in the lives of other family members.

Papa and Mama

My father, Harald Dahl, was a Norwegian who came from a small town near Oslo, called Sarpsborg. His own father, my grandfather, was a fairly prosperous merchant who owned a store in Sarpsborg and traded in just about everything from cheese to chicken-wire.

I am writing these words in 1984, but this grandfather of mine was born, believe it or not, in 1820, shortly after Wellington had defeated Napoleon at Waterloo. If my grandfather had been alive today he would have been one hundred and sixty-four years old. My father would have been one hundred and twenty-one. Both my father and my grandfather were late starters so far as children were concerned.

When my father was fourteen, which is still more than one hundred years ago, he was up on the roof of the family house replacing some loose tiles when he slipped and fell. He broke his left arm below the elbow. Somebody ran to fetch the doctor, and half an hour later this gentleman made a majestic and

Wendy House

Alfhild Ellen and Else me and sister Rodgr

drunken arrival in his horse-drawn buggy. He was so drunk that he mistook the fractured elbow for a dislocated shoulder.

'We'll soon put this back into place!' he cried out, and two men were called off the street to help with the pulling. They were instructed to hold my father by the waist while the doctor grabbed him by the wrist of the broken arm and shouted, 'Pull men, pull! Pull as hard as you can!'

The pain must have been excruciating. The victim screamed, and his mother, who was watching the performance in horror, shouted 'Stop!' But by then the pullers had done so much damage that a splinter of bone was sticking out through the skin of the forearm.

This was in 1877 and orthopaedic surgery was not what it is today. So they simply amputated the arm at the elbow, and for the rest of his life my father had to manage with one arm. Fortunately, it was the left arm that he lost and gradually, over the years, he taught himself to do more or less anything he wanted with just the four fingers and thumb of his right hand. He could tie a shoelace as quickly as you or me, and for cutting up the food on his plate, he sharpened the bottom edge of a fork so that it served as both knife and fork all in one. He kept his ingenious instrument in a slim leather case and carried it in his pocket wherever he went. The loss of an arm, he used to say, caused him only one serious inconvenience. He found it impossible to cut the top off a boiled egg.

My father was a year or so older than his brother Oscar, but they were exceptionally close, and soon after they left school, they went for a long walk together to plan their future. They decided that a small town like Sarpsborg in a small country

like Norway was no place in which to make a fortune. So what they must do, they agreed, was go away to one of the big countries, either to England or France, where opportunities to make good would be boundless.

Their own father, an amiable giant nearly seven feet tall, lacked the drive and ambition of his sons, and he refused to support this tomfool idea. When he forbade them to go, they ran away from home, and somehow or other the two of them managed to work their way to France on a cargo ship.

From Calais they went to Paris, and in Paris they agreed to separate because each of them wished to be independent of the other. Uncle Oscar, for some reason, headed west for La Rochelle on the Atlantic coast, while my father remained in Paris for the time being.

The story of how these two brothers each started a totally separate business in different countries and how each of them made a fortune is interesting, but there is no time to tell it here except in the briefest manner.

Take my Uncle Oscar first. La Rochelle was then, and still is, a fishing port. By the time he was forty he had become the wealthiest man in town. He owned a fleet of trawlers called 'Pêcheurs d'Atlantique' and a large canning factory to can the sardines his trawlers brought in. He acquired a wife from a good family and a magnificent town house as well as a large château in the country. He became a collector of Louis XV furniture, good pictures and rare books, and all these beautiful things together with the two properties are still in the family. I have not seen the château in the country, but I was in the La Rochelle house a couple of years ago and it really is something. The furniture alone should be in a museum.

While Uncle Oscar was bustling around in La Rochelle, his

one-armed brother Harald (my own father) was not sitting on his rump doing nothing. He had met in Paris another young Norwegian called Aadnesen and the two of them now decided to form a partnership and become shipbrokers. A shipbroker is a person who supplies a ship with everything it needs when it comes into port – fuel and food, ropes and paint, soap and towels, hammers and nails, and thousands of other tiddly little items. A shipbroker is a kind of enormous shopkeeper for ships, and by far the most important item he supplies to them

is the fuel on which the ship's engines run. In those days fuel meant only one thing. It meant coal. There were no oil-burning motorships on the high seas at that time. All ships were steamships and these old steamers would take on hundreds and often thousands of tons of coal in one go. To the shipbrokers, coal was black gold.

My father and his new-found friend, Mr Aadnesen, understood all this very well. It made sense they told each other, to set up their shipbroking business in one of the great coal ports of Europe. Which was it to be? The answer was simple. The greatest coaling port in the world at that time was Cardiff, in South Wales. So off to Cardiff they went, these two ambitious young men, carrying with them little or no luggage. But my father had something more delightful then luggage. He had a wife, a young French girl called Marie whom he had recently married in Paris.

In Cardiff, the shipbroking firm of 'Aadnesen & Dahl' was set up and a single room in Bute Street was rented as an office. From then on, we have what sounds like one of those exaggerated fairy-stories of success, but in reality it was the result of tremendous hard and brainy work by those two friends. Very soon 'Aadnesen & Dahl' had more business than the partners could handle alone. Larger office space was acquired and more staff were engaged. The real money then began rolling in. Within a few years, my father was able to buy a fine house in the village of Llandaff, just outside Cardiff, and there his wife Marie bore him two children, a girl and a boy. But tragically, she died after giving birth to the second child.

When the shock and sorrow of her death had begun to subside a little, my father suddenly realized that his two small children ought at the very least to have a stepmother to care for them. What is more, he felt terribly lonely. It was quite obvious that he must try to find himself another wife. But this was easier said than done for a Norwegian living in South Wales who didn't know very many people. So he decided to take a holiday and travel back to his own country, Norway, and who knows, he might if he was lucky find himself a lovely new bride in his own country.

Over in Norway, during the summer of 1911, while taking a trip in a small coastal steamer in the Oslofjord, he met a young lady called Sofie Magdalene Hesselberg. Being a fellow who knew a good thing when he saw one, he proposed to her within a week and married her soon after that.

Harald Dahl took his Norwegian wife on a honeymoon in Paris, and after that back to the house in Llandaff. The two of them were deeply in love and blissfully happy, and during the next six years she bore him four children, a girl, another girl, a boy

Mama Engaged

(me) and a third girl. There were now
six children in the family, two by my
father's first wife and four by his
second. A larger and grander house
was needed and the money was
there to buy it.

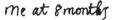
me at 8 months

So in 1918, when I was two, we all
moved into an imposing country
mansion beside the village of Radyr, about
eight miles west of Cardiff. I remember it as a mighty house
with turrets on its roof and with majestic lawns and terraces all
around it. There were many acres of farm and woodland, and
a number of cottages for the staff. Very soon, the meadows
were full of milking cows and the sties were full of pigs and
the chicken-run was full of chickens. There were several
massive shire-horses for pulling the ploughs and the hay-
wagons, and there was a ploughman and a cowman and a
couple of gardeners and all manner of servants in the house
itself. Like his brother Oscar in La Rochelle, Harald Dahl had
made it in no uncertain manner.

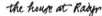
the house at Radyr

But what interests me most of all about these two brothers,
Harald and Oscar, is this. Although they came from a simple

unsophisticated small-town family, both of them, quite independently of one another, developed a powerful interest in beautiful things. As soon as they could afford it, they began to fill their houses with lovely paintings and fine furniture. In addition to that, my father became an expert gardener and above all a collector of alpine plants. My mother used to tell me how the two of them would go on expeditions up into the mountains of Norway and how he would frighten her to death by climbing one-handed up steep cliff-faces to reach small alpine plants growing high up on some rocky ledge. He was also an accomplished wood-carver, and most of the mirror-frames in the house were his own work. So indeed was the entire mantelpiece around the fireplace in the living-room, a splendid design of fruit and foliage and intertwining branches carved in oak.

He was a tremendous diary-writer. I still have one of his many notebooks from the Great War of 1914–18. Every single day during those five war years he would write several pages of comment and observation about the events of the time. He wrote with a pen and although Norwegian was his mother-tongue, he always wrote his diaries in perfect English.

He harboured a curious theory about how to develop a sense of beauty in the minds of his children. Every time my mother became pregnant, he would wait until the last three months of her pregnancy and then he would announce to her that 'the glorious walks' must begin. These glorious walks consisted of him taking her to places of great beauty in the countryside and walking with her for about an hour each day so that she could absorb the splendour of the surroundings. His theory was that if the eye of a pregnant woman was constantly observing the beauty of nature, this beauty would somehome become transmitted to the mind of the unborn baby within her womb and that baby would grow up to be a lover of beautiful things. This was the treatment that all of his children received before they were born.

Reading for meaning

1 How does Roald Dahl make you feel that he is talking directly to you? *Hint: Look at some of the words and phrases he uses and how he explains things that you might not know about.*

2 Dahl sometimes uses humorous **anecdotes** when describing serious events or situations in his father's life. What effect does this have?

3 How is this text different from the Winston Churchill extract? *Hint: Think about the kind of events it describes, the family situation, the language used, and the presentation.*

4 What do you think Roald Dahl wants you to feel about his family? *Hint: Why do you think he begins his **autobiography** with this information about his grandparents, parents and uncle, rather than with details of his own birth?*

5 Why do you think the writer chose to include illustrations? What do they add to your enjoyment of the text?

An **anecdote** is a story about an incident, often used to illustrate a point in an argument or to support a statement about a person's character. Anecdotes are frequently amusing, but may use this to emphasise a serious aspect. For example, the anecdote about Harald Dahl's broken arm has some slapstick comedy in it (that is, the drunken doctor's actions), but the event had a serious outcome for Harald. Roald Dahl uses this anecdote, and others, to show how determined and adaptable his father was.

Keeping track of events

How does Roald Dahl help you keep track of the sequence of events in this text?

a) Make a list of the different ways he does this. Then draw a timeline to show all the events mentioned in the text.

b) Compare your list and timeline with those drawn by another pair. Are there any differences? Work out which is correct, and why.

Vocabulary and spelling

1 Look through this text for examples of words which end '-ent' and '-ant'. Make a note of them in your spelling notebook. Make sure that you know how to spell them by sounding out the separate sounds and syllables, and by memorising the appearance of the words. Add other words with these endings to your lists as you come across them in your work.

2 Roald Dahl ends this chapter of his autobiography with this extract from 'a letter from Papa':

a letter from Papa

The letter reads:

… *the best tonic both for body and brain I should say is plenty of fresh air and exercise. Long deep drafts of sea air before breakfast, in fact before every meal and skipping should beat any chemical concoction.*

Roald Dahl writes in the text that 'although Norwegian was his [father's] mother-tongue, he always wrote … in perfect English'.

Find clues in the letter extract which suggest it was written by some-one whose first language was not English. How would you write those two sentences in modern standard English?

Writing to inform, explain and describe

Write the opening of your own autobiography, using this Roald Dahl text as a model. Your aim is to *inform* readers, to *explain* events and *describe* people from your family to them. You will need to:

- research information about other members of your family and your own early years

- decide which information to use, and how to structure it
  Hint: You could write about events in the order they happened – this is called chronological writing – or you could group information in different ways, for example happy times, sad times, and so on.

- find some suitable photographs or other illustrations

- think carefully about the words you use and the **tone** you create.

Do not try to write too much: about 300–400 words will be enough.

> When we hear words, or read them, we react to the **tone** of those words. The tone may make us like or dislike the speaker or writer, and may influence how far we agree with what is said or written. The tone may be, for example, friendly, aggressive, humorous, bitter, patronising, etc. Tone is created by the speaker's or writer's choice of words and the structure of sentences.

Speaking and listening

Select an interesting incident from your autobiographical writing. Think about how you could retell this as an oral **anecdote** to the class.

You may need to add extra detail, or to repeat or emphasise information in different ways so that listeners can understand and follow what you say. It is harder to take something in if you hear it only once – if you are reading, you can always reread if necessary!

Prepare and rehearse this talk with a partner – it should last about two minutes. Think about the advice you are given, so that when you present your talk to a larger group, it will be as successful as possible. Use this opportunity also to practise listening so that you can offer advice about how your partner might improve her or his talk.

My Family and Other Animals

The last text in this chapter is the opening of Gerald Durrell's *My Family and Other Animals*. The book is a sort of **autobiography**, but the author is more interested in giving an account of the wildlife on Corfu than in writing a detailed account of himself and his family. This extract describes the family's decision to leave England.

My Family and Other Animals

July had been blown out like a candle by a biting wind that ushered in a leaden August sky. A sharp, stinging drizzle fell, billowing into opaque grey sheets when the wind caught it. Along the Bournemouth sea-front the beach-huts turned blank wooden faces towards a greeny-grey, froth-chained sea that leapt eagerly at the cement bulwark of the shore. The gulls had been tumbled inland over the town, and they now drifted above the house-tops on taut wings, whining peevishly. It was the sort of weather calculated to try anyone's endurance.

Considered as a group my family was not a very prepossessing sight that afternoon, for the weather had brought with it the usual selection of ills to which we were prone. For me, lying on the floor, labelling my collection of shells, it had brought catarrh, pouring it into my skull like cement, so that I was forced to breath stertorously through open mouth. For my brother Leslie, hunched dark and glowering by the fire, it had inflamed the convolutions of his ears so that they bled delicately but persistently. To my sister Margo it had delivered a fresh dappling of acne spots to a face that was already blotched like a red veil. For my mother there was a rich, bubbling cold, and a twinge of rheumatism to season it. Only my eldest brother, Larry, was untouched, but it was sufficient that he was irritated by our failings.

It was Larry, of course, who started it. The rest of us felt too apathetic to think of anything except our own ills, but Larry was designed by Providence to go through life like a small, blond firework, exploding ideas in other people's minds, and then curling up with cat-like unctuousness and refusing to take any blame for the consequences. He had become increasingly irritable as the afternoon wore on. At length, glancing moodily round the room, he decided to attack Mother, as being the obvious cause of the trouble.

'Why do we stand this bloody climate?' he asked suddenly, making a gesture towards the rain-distorted window. 'Look at it! And, if it comes to that, look at us. … Margo swollen up like a plate of scarlet porridge … Leslie wandering around with fourteen fathoms of cotton wool in each ear … Gerry sounds as though he's had a cleft palate from birth … And look at you: you're looking more decrepit and hag-ridden every day.'

Mother peered over the top of a large volume entitled *Easy Recipes from Rajputana*.

'Indeed I'm not,' she said indignantly.

'You *are*,' Larry insisted; '… and your family looks like a series of illustrations from a medical encyclopedia.'

Mother could think of no really crushing reply to this, so she contented herself with a glare before retreating once more behind her book.

'What we need is sunshine,' Larry continued; 'don't you agree, Les? … Les … *Les*!'

Leslie unravelled a large quantity of cotton-wool from one ear.

'What d'you say?' he asked.

'There you are!' said Larry, turning triumphantly to Mother, 'it's become a major operation to hold a conversation with him. I ask you, what a position to be in! One brother can't hear what you say, and the other one can't be understood. Really, it's time something was done. I can't be expected to produce deathless prose in an atmosphere of gloom and eucalyptus.'

'Yes, dear,' said Mother vaguely.

'What we all need,' said Larry, getting into his stride again, 'is sunshine … a country where we can *grow*.'

'Yes, dear, that would be nice,' agreed Mother, not really listening.

'I had a letter from George this morning – he says Corfu's wonderful. Why don't we pack up and go to Greece?'

'Very well, dear, if you like,' said Mother unguardedly.

Where Larry was concerned she was generally very careful not to commit herself.

'When?' asked Larry, rather surprised at this cooperation.

Mother, perceiving that she had made a tactical error, cautiously lowered *Easy Recipes from Rajputana*.

'Well, I think it would be a sensible idea if you were to go on ahead, dear, and arrange things. Then you can write and tell me if it's nice, and we all can follow,' she said cleverly.

Larry gave her a withering look.

'You said *that* when I suggested going to Spain,' he reminded her, 'and I sat for two interminable months in Seville, waiting for you to come out, while you did nothing except write me massive letters about drains and drinking-water, as though I was the Town Clerk or something. No, if we're going to Greece, let's all go together.'

'You do *exaggerate*, Larry,' said Mother plaintively; 'anyway, I can't go just like that. I have to arrange something about this house.'

'Arrange? Arrange what, for heaven's sake? Sell it.'

'I can't do that, dear,' said Mother, shocked.

'Why not?'

'But I've only just bought it.'

'Sell it while it's still untarnished, then.'

'Don't be ridiculous, dear,' said Mother firmly; 'that's quite out of the question. It would be madness.'

So we sold the house and fled from the gloom of the English summer, like a flock of migrating swallows.

Reading for meaning

1 Why do you think Gerald Durrell begins his book with a description of the weather?

2 What sort of a person is Larry? *Hint: How does he behave towards his family? What do they seem to think about him? Can you work out what his occupation (or job) is?*

3 What sort of a person is Mother? *Hint: Look at the words used to describe her reactions – and remember the last paragraph!*

4 Is Gerald Durrell's account of this event reliable? *Hint: It was written about 20 years afterwards, and he is trying to be humorous. What effect might this have had on his account?*

5 How does Gerald Durrell try to make this scene amusing? *Hint: Think about the situation, the action and the language.*

Vocabulary

1 How does Gerald Durrell use language in different ways to make you interested? For example, how does he:

- contrast everyday words and **slang** with more **formal language**, for example in dialogue and description?

- use exaggeration?

- use unexpected **imagery**?

Present your findings as a spider diagram.

2 Explain how Gerald Durrell chooses particular words and uses **imagery**, **alliteration** and **personification** to create a particular effect in the first paragraph.

Use quotations to support the points you make.

3 Gerald Durrell writes that, apart from Larry, the family members were 'apathetic'.
a) Find the noun from which this adjective is formed.
b) Find three other nouns and adjectives which show the same pattern. Note their meanings in your spelling notebook.

Imagery describes the vivid use of language to create a particular picture or sense in the reader's mind. **Metaphors** and **similes** are images, but individual words – such as the choice of 'hobbled', 'limped' or 'strode' to describe how someone walked – are also an aspect of imagery. Extended images may be used to emphasise a comparison, as in the extract from *King Henry V* on page 162, when soldiers are compared to ferocious tigers.

Personification is a form of **metaphor** in which non-human objects are described as though they act like humans or show human emotions. This is often used by writers to add a particular atmosphere to their writing. For example, in the first paragraph of this text, Durrell personifies the month, the weather, the beach huts, the sea and the gulls to make it sound as though there is an almost-human conspiracy on the part of nature to make the family want to move away from their dismal surroundings.

Paragraphs

1   How has Gerald Durrell structured this text? Look at:

- the mix of description and dialogue

- the pattern of sentence structures in the second paragraph

- how the dialogue contrasts the characters of Larry and Mother

- the effect of the word 'So' which starts the final paragraph.

2   a)   What is the effect of the first paragraph?

  b)   What is the effect of the second paragraph?

  c)   Explain how they are different.
       Hint: Look at content, tone, length, language.

Punctuation

Gerald Durrell uses a large number of commas in this text. What are some of the different functions they perform?

Writing to analyse, comment and review

Write a letter from Larry to his friend George (who lives on Corfu). In the letter, he describes his feelings about his family and the English weather, and how he wants to go abroad to continue with his writing.

The letter is written after the incident described in this text, when the decision to move to Corfu has been taken.

- *Analyse* the family's reaction to your suggestion.

- *Comment* on how you think you will handle the situation now.

- *Review* the chances of a successful move, given that you have tried before and failed to persuade the family to move to a better climate.

Remember this is an **informal** letter to a friend, so think carefully about what you write and how you write it.

Writing to imagine, explore and entertain

Write a narrative in which the family talk more about the decision to move to Corfu. This takes place the morning after the incident described by Gerald Durrell.

- Involve all the family members mentioned in the text.

- Use dialogue to practise your **punctuation of direct speech.**

- Try to make the characters behave and speak consistently with how Gerald Durrell describes them.

Include some description at the beginning and end to set the scene and to bring it to a suitable conclusion.

This text provides many examples of how to **punctuate speech**. Notice:
- the punctuation that is needed in addition to the actual speech marks (inverted commas) around spoken words
- the unexpected use of lower case letters which can follow a question mark or exclamation mark inside the speech marks.

The convention of starting a new line every time the speaker changes helps the reader understand who is saying what without the need for the writer to keep repeating names.

Review

What did you particularly enjoy in this chapter?

What did you not like very much?

Was there anything:
- you found difficult to understand?
- you discovered or understood for the first time?

Use this checklist to help you answer these questions and to review the progress you have made.

- **You have read:** two modern poems; extracts from a modern children's novel and a fictional diary; extracts from an early twentieth-century autobiography, a modern autobiography, and an autobiographical information text.

- **You have thought about how writers use**: techniques such as rhythm, rhyme, imagery (including similes and metaphors), personification, sound and tone; different text types such as biography and autobiography, fiction and non-fiction, narrative and anecdote.

- **You have written to**: imagine, explore and entertain – a playscript and a narrative; inform, explain and describe – a description and a piece of autobiography; persuade, argue and advise – a letter and a debating speech; analyse, review and comment – a survey and a letter.

- **To improve your writing, you have thought about**: verbs, including the active and passive voice and participles; etymology, including the influence of Latin; formal and informal language, and standard English; features of persuasive writing, including irony and rhetorical questions; using colons and semi-colons.

- **Your speaking and listening work has included**: discussing texts in pairs and as a class; preparing and reading poetry in a group; devising and performing improvised drama; recounting a personal anecdote; evaluating your own and others' work.

- **You may have used ICT to**: tabulate and present the results of a survey and some research; scan illustrations into your work; spellcheck, and present final drafts of your writing neatly and attractively.

2 Journeys and adventures

> This chapter is all about places people visit and journeys they make. It is also about what happens to them on these journeys, some of which change their lives.

Speaking and listening

In groups, discuss the following questions.

Someone in the group will listen to the discussion, noting down the main points ready to give a report back to the class. Someone else will need to be in charge of the discussion, making sure that everyone has a chance to speak.

1 What different sorts of journeys have you made?

2 Why do people go on journeys?

3 What is the first journey you can remember making? Why was it memorable?

4 What other journeys stick in your mind? Why?

5 Talk about a place which made a deep impression on you. Why did it do this?

6 Where do you dream of going if you had the time and lots of money? Why?

2.1 Poetry

The Way Through the Woods

Sometimes a place we visit may make us think about others who have been there before us. Many people who visit Hadrian's Wall, for example, wonder what it would have been like to march across the bleak northern landscape and to live in one of its windblown forts as a Roman soldier almost two thousand years ago.

The first text in this section is a poem by Rudyard Kipling about a road that has disappeared. Maybe this was once a Roman road, but now it is buried beneath a wood. The speaker in the poem imagines some of the sounds that were made by travellers on the vanished road.

Before you read

1   What are deserted or forgotten places like? How do they make you feel when you are there?

2   What sort of places make you think particularly about the past? What feelings do they give you?

3   If you could have lived in a different historical period, which one would you choose? What do you imagine it was like?

THE WAY THROUGH THE WOODS

They shut the road through the woods
Seventy years ago.
Weather and rain have undone it again,
And now you would never know
There was once a road through the woods   5
Before they planted the trees.
It is underneath the coppice and heath
And the thin anemones.
Only the keeper sees
That, where the ring-dove broods,   10
And the badgers roll at ease,
There was once a road through the woods.

Yet, if you enter the woods
Of a summer evening late,
When the night-air cools on the trout-ringed pools   15
Where the otter whistles his mate,
(They fear not men in the woods,
Because they see so few.)
You will hear the beat of a horse's feet.
And the swish of a skirt in the dew,   20
Steadily cantering through
The misty solitudes,
As though they perfectly knew
The old lost road through the woods …
But there is no road through the woods.   25

Reading for meaning

1 Who might 'they' be (lines 1 and 6)?

2 Why do you think the wildlife in the wood is described in such detail?

3 What does the word 'broods' mean (line 10)? *Hint: It has more than one possible meaning!*

4 What is the speaker describing in lines 19–24?

5 What does the speaker seem to feel about the change that has taken place in the wood?

Empathy literally means 'feeling with', and it describes how you identify with, or are able to see a situation through the eyes of, a character in a text. This could apply to seeing the viewpoint of a historical character in a non-fiction text, such as one of the crew members of the *Titanic* whose actions are described in a later text, or understanding the feelings of a fictional character, such as the person speaking in this poem.

Kipling's poetic technique

1 How are you made to feel as if the poem is being spoken directly to you?

2 What words and phrases are repeated? How does repetition add to its meaning and effect?

3 Why do you think there is an 'extra' 13th line at the end of the second stanza?

4 How is rhyme used in this poem? *Hint: Look within lines as well as the ends of lines.*

5 How do the **rhythm** and **sounds** in this poem add to the atmosphere? *Hint: Look back at page 24 if you are unsure about this.*

Travel writing

The Titanic

On the morning of 10 April 1912, a ship sailed from Southampton with 2,235 passengers and crew bound for New York. The *Titanic* was huge, the size of a cathedral, and as luxurious as the finest hotel. It was a modern wonder of the world, a symbol of the future – and everyone thought it was unsinkable.

Before you read

1 What do you already know about the *Titanic*?

2 Why do you think the *Titanic* is still remembered, nearly one hundred years after it sank?

3 Why you think people are so interested in travel disasters?

Reading for meaning

When you have read the text, answer these questions.

1 Why do you think the writer begins this account with details of the ship's mileage and speed?

2 How does the writer create a sense of possible danger before the ship actually strikes the iceberg?

3 Why do you think the writer chose to mention the events described in the paragraph beginning 'Within ten minutes …'?

4 a) What does this sentence mean: 'There is going to be no coherent account of what happened in the last hour of the *Titanic*, because nothing coherent happened.'?

   b) How does the rest of the account illustrate it?

5 Does this account differ in any way from other versions you know of the sinking of the *Titanic*? What are the differences? How do they affect the way you react to the disaster?

The Titanic

From Thursday noon to Friday noon the *Titanic* ran 386 nautical miles. Friday to Saturday 519 miles, and Saturday to Sunday 546 miles. She was making 22 knots. Everyone agreed she was the most comfortable ship they had travelled in. There was, though, a vibration, which was most noticeable as one lay in the bath. The throb of the engines came straight up from the floor through the metal sides of the tub so that one could not put one's head back with any comfort. Throughout her voyage, the *Titanic* slightly listed to port, but it was nothing. As the second-class passengers sat at table in the dining-room they could, if they watched the skyline through the portholes, see both skyline and sea on the port side but only sky to starboard. The purser thought this was probably because more coal had been used from the starboard bunkers.

When some passengers went on deck on Sunday morning they found the temperature had dropped so rapidly that they did not care to stay outside, although there was no wind, or only that artificial wind created by the passage of the ship. Both the French liner *Touraine* and the German *Amerika* had wire-lessed the *Titanic* reporting ice, and the *Titanic* had replied thanking them. Sunday dinner was served, and then coffee. Thomas Andrews, the shipbuilder, strolled down to the kitchens to thank the baker for making some special bread for him. The passengers went to bed with the presumption, perhaps already mentally half-realised, as (Lawrence) Beesley put it, that they would be ashore in New York in forty-eight hours time. At the evening service, after coffee, Rev. Mr Carter had caused the hymn 'For Those in Peril on the Sea' to be sung, but he had brought the service to a close with a few words on the great confidence all on board felt in the *Titanic*'s great steadiness and size. At 11.40, in Lat. 41° 46′ N. Long. 50° 14′ W. Frederick Fleet, the look-out in the crow's-nest, saw or sensed an iceberg ahead. The

Titanic veered to port, so that it was her starboard plates which were glanced open. The engines were stopped. There was a perfectly still atmosphere. It was a brilliantly starlit night but with no moon, so that there was little light that was of any use. She was a ship that had come quietly to rest without any indication of disaster. No ice was visible: the iceberg had been glimpsed by the look-out and then gone. There was no hole in the ship's side through which water could be seen to be pouring, nothing out of place, no sound of alarm, no panic, and no movement of anyone except at a walking pace.

Within ten minutes the water had risen fourteen feet inside the ship. Mail bags were floating about in the mail room. The passengers had no idea of danger. Beesley, who was in bed, noticed no more than what he took to be the slightest extra heave of the engines. What most people noticed first was the sudden lack of engine vibration. This had been with them so constantly for the four days of the voyage that they had ceased to be conscious of it, but when it stopped they noticed the supervening silence and stillness. The only passengers who saw an iceberg were a few still playing cards in the smoking room. They idly discussed how high it might have been, settled on an estimate of eighty feet, and went back to their cards. One pointed to a glass of whisky at his side and, turning to an onlooker, suggested he should just run along on deck to see if any ice had come on board. If so, he would like some more in his whisky. They laughed. In fact, as the crew discovered, the decks were strewn with ice, but even then, so unaware were they of danger, that Edward Buley, an able seaman, picked up a handful of it, took it down to his bunk, and turned in again. There was no panic because there was no awareness. The *Titanic* was assumed to be unsinkable. The shipbuilders had said so. Practically everyone believed she was as unsinkable as a railway station. A Rothschild, asked to put on his life-jacket, said he did not think there was any occasion for it, and walked leisurely away.

Stewards rode bicycles round and round in the gym. She was in fact sinking very fast, and by midnight was a quarter sunk already. There was something unusual about the stairs, a curious sense of something out of balance, a sense of not being able to put one's foot down in the right place. The stairs were tilting forward and tended to throw your feet out of place. There was no visible slope, just something strange perceived by the sense of balance. The *Titanic* was settling by the head.

There is going to be no coherent account of what happened in the last hour of the *Titanic*, because nothing coherent happened. The *Titanic* was a sixth of a mile long and had eleven decks. What happened in one place did not happen in another. What happened on the starboard side did not happen on the port. On the port side, women and children only were allowed into the boats which were even sent away half-empty when there were not women enough at that moment to fill them, although there were men. On the starboard side, men were allowed to enter the boats when there were not at any given moment enough women to fill them. There was even a difference of opinion as to what constituted a woman. Second Officer Lightoller took any women, except stewardesses. Fifth Officer Lowe accepted any women, 'whether first class, second class, third class, or sixty-seventh class … regardless of class or nationality or pedigree. Stewardesses just the same.' Lowe, however, said he fended off a lot of Italian men. Latin people, all along the ship's rails, 'more or less like wild beasts, ready to spring'. But the severe Lightoller saw none of this, and said that the men whom he refused to allow into his boats 'could not have stood quieter if they had been in church'. Major Arthur Peuchen, who held his commission in the Canadian militia and got away into a boat because he was a yachtsman and could help to handle it, saw a hundred stokers with their bags crowd a whole deck in front of the boats until an officer he did not recognise, a very powerful man, drove them right off the deck like a lot of sheep. Others said not a soul emerged from the engine room. Certainly no single engineer survived. Lowe said they were never seen.

Everyone agrees that the band played until the last. There were eight of them, and none survived. They had played throughout dinner and then gone to their berths. About twenty to one, when the ship was foundering, the cellist ran down the deserted starboard deck, his cello trailing behind him with the spike dragging along the floor. Soon after that the band began to play ragtime. They were still playing ragtime when the last boat was launched.

Colonel Astor, having placed his young bride in one of the boats, lit a cigarette and looked over the rails. Benjamin Guggenheim changed into evening dress, saying that if he had to die he would die like a gentleman. Thomas Andrews leaned against a mantelpiece in the smoking room. A steward asked him, 'Aren't you going to try for it, sir?' He did not reply. John Collins, aged seventeen, an assistant cook making his first sea voyage, saw the stewards with their white jackets steering some passengers along, making a joke of it. One steward was helping a woman with two children. The steward was carrying one child and the woman the other. Collins took the child the woman was carrying. 'Then,' he said, 'the sailors and the firemen that were forward seen the ship's bow in the water and seen that she was intending to sink her bow, and they shouted out for all they were worth we were to go aft, and we were just turning round and making for the stern when the wave washed us off the deck, washed us clear of it, and the child was washed out of my arms: and the wreckage, and the people that was around me, they kept me down for at least two or three minutes under the water.' The sea was calm as a board, but when the bow went under the water it created a wave that washed the decks clear, and there were hundreds on it.

These are the detailed figures for survivors given in the report of the British Board of Trade inquiry:

	Number on board	Number saved	Percentage saved
First-class passengers			
Men	173	58	34
Women	144	139	97
Children	5	5	10
Second-class passengers			
Men	160	13	8
Women	93	78	84
Children	24	24	100
Third-class passengers			
Men	454	55	12
Women	179	98	55
Children	76	25	30
Total passengers	1308	493	38
Crew	898	210	23
Total	2206	703	32

Taking each class of passenger as a whole, of the first class 63 per cent were saved, of the second class 42 per cent, and of the third class 23 per cent.

Fact and opinion

1 Would you expect a text like this to be mainly **fact** or mainly **fiction**? Why?

2 What are facts, and what are **opinions**, guesses or estimates in this account? How do you know?

3 Why do writers sometimes create fictional accounts of historical events such as the sinking of the *Titanic*?

A **fact** is something which can be supported by evidence, for example the figures Terry Coleman gives in the first three sentences of this text, which could be checked from shipping records.

An **opinion** is a belief for which there is no evidence available, or for which there could never be definite evidence, for example when Terry Coleman writes 'Everyone agreed she was the most comfortable ship they had travelled in.'

Vocabulary

a) With a partner, find and list the technical words and phrases to do with ships and the sea in this text.

b) Create a table which lists the terms alphabetically and gives a definition of the meaning of each.

c) Under the table, list your sources of information and add a paragraph which explains why you think the writer chose to use these specialist terms.

Language variation

Look at the words spoken by John Collins in the last paragraph.

a) What can you say about the **verb** form 'seen' in the first few lines?

b) What can you say about the verb form in this phrase: 'the people that was around me'? *Hint: What would the **standard English** forms be? Why might he have used these forms?*

Writing to inform, explain and describe

Write the diary entries of two passengers who survived the sinking of the *Titanic*.

- One of the passengers is someone who had been travelling First Class.

- The other someone who had been travelling Third Class.

Bring out the different experiences they had in escaping from the ship. Include their thoughts about the disaster in general, as well as details of their own escape.

Make sure that you use some incidents described in this text as well as using your imagination.

Writing to analyse, review and comment

Write an *analysis* of the table at the end of the text (on page 71) which shows the detailed figures for survivors. *Review* the information it gives, and *comment* on the conclusions you can draw from it, such as:

- the survival rates of passengers travelling in different classes

- what difference it made to be a man, woman or child

- how the chances of the crew compared with those of passengers.

Drama

One of the ship's officers is trying to organise the loading of a lifeboat. Improvise this short scene.

In your preparation:

- decide on the roles to be played by different members of the group

- agree which details from the text you will use

- decide what else you will need to imagine or invent

- think about how you will begin and end your scene effectively.

Use the evaluation sheet to record comments about your own group's work, and the performances given by other groups.

Far-away places

Now that modern transport and tourist developments have opened up most of the world to travellers, newspapers and magazines are full of advertisements for far-flung holidays like those on page 75 and 76.

Reading for meaning

When you have read the advertisements, answer these questions.

1   Why is it impossible to tell from these advertisements exactly how much the holidays would cost you? *Hint: Look at the small print!*

2   Once you have arrived at your first destination, what different methods of transport are then used on the two holidays?

3   If you particularly enjoyed (a) swimming in the sea or (b) horse riding, which holiday would suit you better? How long would each holiday last? *Hint: Read very carefully to work out the length of stay!*

4   If you were equally interested in both holidays, but could only go away in February 2001, which holiday would be better value? *Hint: Does better value just mean the cheaper price? If not, what else will you take into account?*

5   Name three ways you could find out more about these holidays.

Vocabulary

1   How do the titles of the two advertisements try to attract your attention? *Hint: Look at the words chosen, and any literary devices used.*

2   How has the writer of 'The Amazon Experience' advertisement made it seem that it is addressed directly to you?

3   What sort of person do you think is most likely to be interested in the 'Oriental Odyssey' advertisement?

4   What different descriptions of hotel quality are used in the advertisements? What do these descriptions tell you about the hotels?

5   Find three adjectives in each advertisement. Explain how each is intended to make an aspect or feature of the holiday sound especially enjoyable.

from £899

The Amazon Experience

A River Trip in the Amazon Rainforest of Ecuador, plus Quito 8 nights

Our journey takes us to Ecuador and its Amazon River region for 3 nights on the Aguarico River. Along the river lies the Cuyabeno Wildlife Reserve where the jungle is home to some of the region's most fascinating animals and over 500 species of birds.

Day 1 London/Quito
4 nights at the superior medium class Radisson Hotel in Quito.
Day 2 - Day 4 Quito
Included are a city tour and a visit to the Otavalo area: buy an authentic Panama hat – yes they really are made in Ecuador!
Day 5 Quito/Cuyabeno Reserve
Fly to Lago Agrio, then by road to the Aguarico Amazon tributary. Then by motorboat ($2^{1}/_{2}$ hours) to the Flotel Orellana for a 3 night stay. On 3 decks, this charming, flat-bottomed ship has 22 cabins opening onto the deck. Cabins are cooled by electric fans and have upper/lower berths, private shower and wc. Daily excursions into the jungle, on foot and by canoe.
Day 6 Cuyabeno Wildlife Reserve
A guided walk through the forest to a hilltop observation tower.

Enjoy a tasty 'Jungle Barbecue' for lunch. The more adventurous may choose to spend the night in a simple camp in the care of an expert guide.
Day 7 Cuyabeno Wildlife Reserve
Visit a 'Cofani' village and travel along the river in a dugout canoe, ideal for birdwatching.
Day 8 Cuyabeno/Quito
Return by boat and by road to Lago Agrio for the flight to Quito. Transfer to the Radisson Hotel, Quito.
Day 9 Quito/London
Flight to London. Or an optional 'Hacienda and Highlands' extension: 3 nights at the 18th century Hacienda La Carriona. 31 rooms, swimming pool, sauna and horse riding. From £99 extra (inc breakfast/dinner).

THE PRICE INCLUDES:
Scheduled flights. Full breakfast in hotel. All meals on Flotel. Excursions/sightseeing as described. UK Govt dep tax of £20. Prices per person sharing twin.
(Single supp: from £99)
Not included: Local dep tax.
Guide/crew gratuities.
Optional insurance: £33
(8 nights); £55 (9 nights or more).
Booking conditions apply.

Dates and Prices

Departures:	Price:
23 Nov 2000	£949
30 Nov, 07 Dec	£899
18 Jan 2001	£949
01, 15 Feb	£999
08, 22 Mar	£949
12 Apr	£1049
26 Apr	£949
10 May	£949
14, 28 Jun	£899

from £899

Oriental Odyssey

The Great Wall, the Terracotta Army, Shanghai, Canton, Hong Kong & Bangkok. Optional beach stay

The Great Wall of China, the Forbidden City, the Terracotta Army – are all included in this special 12 night holiday which begins in Beijing and travels to Xian and Shanghai; then to Canton and a journey on the famous Canton to Hong Kong Railway; continuing to the exotic Thai capital, Bangkok. From just £99 extra, spend 5 nights at the Thai beach resort of Cha Am.

Day 1 London/Beijing
Depart Heathrow.
Day 2 Beijing
Arrive Beijing. 3 night stay.
Days 3-4 Beijing
Full day tour to the Great Wall, stretching across the hills as far as the eye can see. En route, visit the Ming Tombs. Half day tour to the Forbidden City, for centuries the domain of the Emperors.
Day 5 Beijing/Xian
Fly to Xian for a 2 night stay.
Day 6 Xian
See the magnificent Terracotta Army, with its rank upon rank of soldiers and horsemen on eternal guard over their long-dead Emperor.

Day 7 Xian/Shanghai
Fly to Shanghai. 2 night stay. The city offers a fascinating insight into both old and new China.
Day 9 Shanghai/Canton
Fly to Canton. Overnight stay.
Day 10 Canton/Hong Kong
Depart Canton by train to Hong Kong's Hung Hom station. Transfer for a 2 night stay.
Day 11 Hong Kong
Time to explore on your own.
Day 12 Hong Kong/Bangkok
Fly to Bangkok for 2 nights. Explore the markets and temples of this fascinating city.
Day 14 Bangkok/London
Flight to Heathrow, or you may choose to extend your holiday at the 1st class Regent Hotel, Cha Am from £99 extra.

Dates and Prices

Departures:	Price:
07 Dec 2000	£899
04 Jan 2001	£899
15 Feb	£949
15 Mar	£999
01 Apr	£1,099
17 May, 21 Jun	£1,049
19 Jul	£1,099
16 Aug	£1,149

Hotels: 1st class in Beijing, Xian, Bangkok, Cha Am, medium class elsewhere.

THE PRICE INCLUDES:
Return Scheduled flts. UK Govt dept tax: £20.12 nts accom. China: 8 b-fasts, 2 lunches.Hong Kong/Thailand: no meals. Excursions as described with English speaking guide.
Transfers
Prices per person sharing twin.
Not included: China visa.
Local dept taxes.
Optional insurance: £55.
Booking conditions apply.

Layout and presentation

1 On the worksheet, label and describe the layout features which you can see in both advertisements.

2 Look at the illustrations chosen for the two advertisements.
   a) Why do you think these particular illustrations have been chosen?
   b) Are they likely to attract the people who would enjoy the holiday in each case?

3 How effective overall are these advertisements? *Hint: Think about how eye-catching they are, how appealing the descriptions are, how easy it is to find the information you need, etc.*

Writing to persuade, argue and advise

Using the advertisements you have studied as a model, create a similar advertisement for a holiday in a place that you know well. This could either be a serious advertisement, or a joke (for example, offering a stay in your school!).

The **audience** is the group of people for whom a text is created, in other words, listeners, readers, viewers or users of the Internet. Writers and speakers need to think about the audience for their text if it is to be successful in its purpose. For example, the writers and designers of the advertisements on page 75 and 76 have made certain assumptions about the visits and activities certain people will want to have provided for them.

A Beginning and an End

The last text in this section is about a happy and successful short sea journey – nothing like the *Titanic* crossing the Atlantic! As a child, Leslie Thomas lived in South Wales. He sometimes visited North Devon on holiday and had seen the island of Lundy as something 'distant ... wonderful, mysterious'. When he decided to write about British islands, Lundy therefore seemed the obvious place to start.

Before you read

1 Why do you think some people are so fascinated by islands?

2 What might it be like to live permanently on a small offshore island, where there are very few people and little contact with the outside world?

3 What do you expect a piece of travel writing to be like? Think about:

- the content (what it says)

- the style (how it says it)

- the different purposes and **audiences** there might be for travel writing.

Reading for meaning

When you have read the text, answer these questions.

1 What made Leslie Thomas so keen to go to Lundy?

2 How does Leslie Thomas create a sense of his excitement during his voyage to Lundy? *Hint: What does he do, see, hear and think? What words does he use?*

3 How is Leslie Thomas different from the other day-trippers to Lundy? *Hint: Think about why he has gone there, and what he does when he is there.*

4 The last paragraph describes various people as the day draws to an end. What different feelings do they have, and why?

5 What does the title of this text mean? *Hint: It is the first chapter in the book from which it is taken; and 'end' can have more than one meaning.*

A Beginning and an End

It was Lundy that began it. Lundy, the tubby island, the blue whale of the Bristol Channel.

As a schoolboy I had seen it out on the distant water, fat, wonderful, mysterious. I had seen it both from the head of Devon and the foot of Wales. Always it looked blue and I wondered at what point on the voyage out there the blue turned to green. Or perhaps, I thought, it did not change; that when you arrived it really was an island of deep blue. What a thing that would have been! In those days they used to say, on both the top and bottom sides of the Channel, that if you could see Lundy it was going to rain, and if you couldn't see it then it was already raining.

It was years before I went to my childhood island. Before I made that little voyage I was to stand on islands in the China Sea, in the Indies, in the Caribbean and many other places. They were hot and tropical with idle beaches and palms. But before I went to Lundy I had never been on a *real* island. …

The day I first went there it was with summer at its highest. For a week, every morning, I had been going with my children down to the beach at Croyde in North Devon and there she was out there in the ocean sunshine, blue and big as ever. I gazed at her as I had done when I was a boy. Then, on the second Monday I could stand it no longer. I abandoned the family, jumped into my car and drove like mad to Ilfracombe where I was the last one that morning to buy a ticket for the day trip to Lundy Island. After I'd got my change the lady pulled down the shutter of the little wooden box office with the finality of a guillotine. With my ticket in my hand I went up the gangplank of the pleasure steamer and they pulled it in right after me. You can't leave it any later than that.

I remembered these pleasure boats. Campbells. Before the war they used to run paddle steamers from Newport, down the cocoa Usk to distant and exotic places like Weston-super-Mare, which sounded like Hollywood (and still does). But my mother had discouraged me from anything connected with the sea because the family for generations had all been sailors and, in her opinion, not one of them had come to any good. So I never went.

But here I was, on this brilliant morning in my thirty-second year, voyaging to Lundy with three hundred trippers who broiled under the Bristol Channel sun, licked ice cream and drank pop. Children ran about the deck and mothers screamed. Men put handkerchiefs over their heads. The ship's loudspeaker was playing maritime music and right opposite me two young lovers were going near the bounds of decency, even midsummer decency, on a life-raft capable (it said) of saving fourteen souls.

I cared nothing, I heard nothing, I saw nothing. Nothing, that is, but that blue hump on the top of the sea getting closer, and if anything bluer. I watched it with as much intensity as if I had been alone on the pleasure boat, or for that matter clinging to a lump of cork and on my last castaway gasp. Say it did stay blue! That would be a laugh, not to mention a shock. But no, it couldn't be or the word would have got around.

Nevertheless my careful recollection of that morning was that it didn't turn colour until we were less than a mile away, and then it became rock-grey topped with green.

We went alongside it like one small ship edging close to a big one. At the southern anchorage there was a lighthouse looking strangely like a policeman. Later that day I asked one of the lighthouse men how you clean the windows of a lighthouse and he said you clean them like any other windows, with a chamois leather and a bucket of water. I didn't believe him and I still don't, but at all the lighthouses I've visited since I've never had the nerve to ask the question again in case I get the same answer.

They send out little boats to take you ashore on Lundy because there is no landing stage. They drop you on the beach and when they dropped me I simply stood there for a moment and looked quietly. Kids were charging about and ramming spades into the innocent sand, dads were shouting about picnic baskets and mums were trying to get out of the tender boats without showing their knickers. But I merely stood. For this was an island, a *true* island, not one of those sticky palm-tree places. And at last I was on it.

It was a marvellous day, hot all the time, with birds flying about and such a limitless sky for them too. At the top of the first cliff path I looked down at my boat, far more elegant from above, placed royally on a sea of August blue, with the small tenders making seams in the water as they went back and forth with more passengers.

Somehow I lost everyone else. All three hundred of them, or whatever the number was. Some of them, I heard later, never moved from the beach because older or wearier mums and dads couldn't manage the cliff path. Certainly not many went beyond the village and the post office. … You couldn't blame them because it was very hot.

But I went on, across the bounding grass, over the quarter wall, the halfway wall, and the three-quarter wall, to the old middle lighthouse and the newer one at the northern nose of the island. I had the whole place to myself. I could see South Wales and imagine myself back there, looking over here all those years ago. Well, it wasn't blue. That was settled anyway. Any Welsh or Devonian child who thinks Lundy is blue should make a note of this.

I saw seals for the first time in my life, far below on the sea-washed rocks, and I had the screams of the seabirds in my ears for a long time; in fact they are still there now. Then I poked about among the coves and caves of the pirates and smugglers who used this as a terminus in the far days. I had a bottle of beer and some sandwiches sitting on a giddy clifftop. I got so sunburned that my face peeled for days.

When I went back to the south anchorage the children were crying because they had to leave their sandcastles. Dads were clouting their ears, mothers were collecting bits into baskets and then trying to clamber into the little boats without showing their knickers. The lighthouse men waved, no doubt with relief, and we sailed grandly for Ilfracombe again with me standing at the stern watching the island return to blue in the evening.

Slang describes words or phrases used in informal speech or writing, which may be associated with particular regions, age groups, historical times or social classes. Leslie Thomas's reference to children as 'kids' and fizzy drink as 'pop' are examples of slang.

Vocabulary and spelling

1 In the first paragraph, Leslie Thomas describes Lundy as 'the tubby island; the blue whale'.
   a) What impression of the place, and of his thoughts about it, do these words give you?
   b) Where are there links to these words later in the text? What effect do these links achieve?

2 How do the words and images used in the last two sentences of the fourth paragraph (from 'After I'd got my change …' to '… any later than that.') reflect Leslie Thomas's feelings at that moment?

3 What do the following words mean, and why do you think the writer has chosen them:
   a) idle? (page 79, paragraph 3)
   b) cocoa? (page 80, paragraph 2)
   c) broiled? (page 80, paragraph 3)
   d) innocent? (page 81, paragraph 3)
   e) royally? (page 81, paragraph 4)
   f) seams? (page 81, paragraph 4)
   g) nose? (page 82, paragraph 1)
   h) giddy? (page 82, paragraph 2)

4 a) What meaning does the prefix 'dis-' have in the word 'discourage'? Think of other words with this prefix. What do they mean?
   b) What prefix gives the opposite meaning? Think of some words with this prefix. What do they mean?

5 What meaning and effect is achieved by the repetitions of the word nothing in paragraph seven ('I cared nothing …')?

Sentences, paragraphs and punctuation

1   Look at the last two sentences in paragraph five ('But my mother ... I never went.'). What can you say about the structure and effect of these sentences? *Hint: Look at the use of subordinate clauses, connectives, sentence length.*

2   a)   How is the last paragraph of the text related to the two earlier paragraphs which begin 'We went alongside ...' and 'They send out little boats ...'? *Hint: Look at what these paragraphs describe, and the language used.*

    b)   Why do you think the writer made these links?

    c)   What other typical features of a recount text can you find in this piece?

3   How does Leslie Thomas make his style of writing seem friendly and conversational? *Hint: Think about his use of* **contractions**, **slang** *and how he often starts sentences with words such as 'but' and 'or'.*

A **contraction** is:
- a word which has been shortened, such as 'mum' = 'mother', or
- two words which have been made into one, for example 'I'd' = 'I had' or 'didn't' = 'did not'.

Contraction is a common feature of spoken language, and may be used in writing to give an informal or more friendly feel.

Writing to inform, explain and describe

Write a *description* of a place which you enjoyed visiting as much as Leslie Thomas did Lundy. Make sure that you:

- *inform* your readers about the place: where it is, what its main features are, and so on

- *explain* your feelings about the place, and why you have them.

2.3 A short story

The Gold Cadillac

This is a complete short story by the American writer Mildred D. Taylor. It is about a special family trip, one which would never be forgotten. On the surface, the story is about a journey in a special car, but the real theme is the **symbolic** journey made by the story-teller and her family in coming to understand the society they live in.

The story is divided into four parts so you can stop and think about the writer's ideas and methods.

Before you read

1   Why do you think fiction writers often include journeys in their narratives? *Hint: Think about* **symbolism**.

2   What other stories describe an important journey? *Hint: Do you know any fables, nursery rhymes or any Greek or Roman* **myths**?

3   What does the title of the story, 'The Gold Cadillac', suggest to you? *Hint: What about gold? And Cadillac?*

Symbolism is when a person, object, event or place represents something else in addition to its obvious, surface meaning. In 'The Gold Cadillac', the car symbolises the father's desire to be seen as a success, *and* the disagreement between the parents. The journey symbolises the inner journey they make in coming to realise some truths about their society.

A **myth** is an ancient traditional story which has a message. Myths are usually about gods and heroes, a significant problem in daily life or they explain a natural phenomenon, such as thunder and lightning.

The Gold Cadillac

My sister and I were playing out on the front lawn when the gold Cadillac rolled up and my father stepped from behind the wheel. We ran to him, our eyes filled with wonder. 'Daddy, whose Cadillac?' I asked.

And Wilma demanded, 'Where's our Mercury?'

My father grinned. 'Go get your mother and I'll tell you all about it.'

'Is it ours?' I cried. 'Daddy, is it ours?'

'Get your mother!' he laughed. 'And tell her to hurry!'

Wilma and I ran off to obey as Mr Pondexter next door came from his house to see what this new Cadillac was all about. We threw open the front door, ran through the downstairs front parlour and straight through the house to the kitchen where my mother was cooking and one of my aunts was helping her. 'Come on, Mother-Dear!' we cried together. 'Daddy say come on out and see this new car!'

'What?' said my mother, her face showing her surprise. 'What're you talking about?'

'A Cadillac!' I cried.

'He said hurry up!' relayed Wilma.

And then we took off again, up the back stairs to the second floor of the duplex. Running down the hall, we banged on all the apartment doors. My uncles and their wives stepped to the doors. It was good it was a Saturday morning. Everybody was home.

'We got us a Cadillac! We got us a Cadillac!' Wilma and I proclaimed in unison. We had decided that the Cadillac had to be ours if our father was driving it and holding on to the keys. 'Come on see!' Then we raced on, through the upstairs sunroom, down the front steps. through the downstairs sunroom, and out to the Cadillac. Mr Pondexter was still there. Mr LeRoy and Mr Courtland from down the street were there too and all were admiring the Cadillac as my father stood proudly by, pointing out the various features.

'Brand–new 1950 Coup de Ville!' I heard one of the men saying.

'Just off the showroom floor!' my father said. 'I just couldn't resist it.'

My sister and I eased up to the car and peeked in. It was all gold inside. Gold leather seats. Gold carpeting. Gold dashboard. It was like no car we had owned before. It looked like a car for rich folks.

'Daddy, are we rich?' I asked. My father laughed.

'Daddy, it's ours, isn't it?' asked Wilma, who was older and more practical than I. She didn't intend to give her heart too quickly to something that wasn't hers.

'You like it?'

'Oh, Daddy, yes!'

He looked at me. 'What 'bout you, 'lois?'

'Yes, sir!'

My father laughed again. 'Then I expect I can't much disappoint my girls, can I? It's ours all right!'

Wilma and I hugged our father with our joy. My uncles came from the house and my aunts, carrying their babies, came out too. Everybody surrounded the car and owwed and ahhed. Nobody could believe it.

Then my mother came out.

Everybody stood back grinning as she approached the car. There was no smile on her face. We all waited for her to speak. She stared at the car, then looked at my father, standing there as proud as he could be. Finally she said, 'You didn't buy this car, did you, Wilbert?'

'Gotta admit I did. Couldn't resist it.'

'But … but what about our Mercury? It was perfectly good!'

'Don't you like the Cadillac, Dee?'

'That Mercury wasn't even a year old!'

My father nodded. 'And I'm sure whoever buys it is going to get themselves a good car. But we've got ourselves a better one. Now stop frowning, honey, and let's take ourselves a ride in our brand-new Cadillac!'

My mother shook her head. 'I've got food on the stove,' she said and turning away walked back to the house.

There was an awkward silence and then my father said, 'You know Dee never did much like surprises. Guess this here Cadillac was a bit too much for her. I best go smooth things out with her.'

Everybody watched as he went after my mother. But when he came back, he was alone.

'Well, what she say?' asked one of my uncles.

My father shrugged and smiled. 'Told me I bought this Cadillac alone, I could just ride in it alone.'

Another uncle laughed. 'Uh-oh! Guess she told you!'

'Oh, she'll come around,' said one of my aunts. 'Any woman would be proud to ride in this car.'

'That's what I'm banking on,' said my father as he went around to the street side of the car and opened the door. 'All right! Who's for a ride?'

'We are!' Wilma and I cried.

All three of my uncles and one of my aunts, still holding her baby, and Mr Pondexter climbed in with us and we took off for the first ride in the gold Cadillac. It was a glorious ride and we drove all through the city of Toledo. We rode past the church and past the school. We rode through Ottawa Hills where the rich folks lived and on into Walbridge Park and past the zoo, then along the Maumee River. But none of us had had enough of the car so my father put the car on the road and we drove all the way to Detroit. We had plenty of family there and everybody was just as pleased as could be about the Cadillac. My father told our Detroit relatives that he was in the doghouse with my mother about buying the

Cadillac. My uncles told them she wouldn't ride in the car. All the Detroit family thought that was funny and everybody, including my father, laughed about it and said my mother would come around.

It was early evening by the time we got back home, and I could see from my mother's face she had not come around. She was angry now not only about the car, but that we had been gone so long. I didn't understand that, since my father had called her as soon as we reached Detroit to let her know where we were. I had heard him myself. I didn't understand either why she did not like that fine Cadillac and thought she was being terribly disagreeable with my father. That night as she tucked Wilma and me in bed I told her that too.

'Is this your business?' she asked.

'Well, I just think you ought to be nice to Daddy. I think you ought to ride in that car with him! It'd sure make him happy.'

'I think you ought to go to sleep,' she said and turned out the light.

Later I heard her arguing with my father. 'We're supposed to be saving for a house!' she said.

'We've already got a house!' said my father.

'But you said you wanted a house in a better neighbourhood. I thought that's what we both said!'

'I haven't changed my mind.'

'Well, you have a mighty funny way of saving for it, then. Your brothers are saving for houses of their own and you don't see them out buying new cars every year!'

'We'll still get the house, Dee. That's a promise!'

'Not with new Cadillacs we won't!' said my mother and then she said a very loud good night and all was quiet.

Reading for meaning

1 How are the storyteller's father and mother shown to be different through what they say and do?

2 What do you learn about the family's home, their surroundings and their way of life (for example, how well-off they are, how they spend their time)?

3 Why did father buy the car, and why was mother so angry about it?

4 What are the differences between the storyteller and her sister, Wilma? What does each of them feel about the situation caused by the new car?

5 How does the writer make it seem that the story is being told through the eyes of a child? *Hint: Look at* what *she chooses to describe, and* how *she describes these things*.

USA English
- Some words used in USA English are not used at all in the UK. For example, in the first section of this text, what is a 'duplex'? In the second section, what is a 'gas station' and a 'drugstore'?
- Words that look familiar may have a different meaning when used in the USA. For example, look for the word 'caravan' in this text, and see if you can work out what it means. *Hint: It was used with a very similar meaning in the extract from* Children on the Oregon Trail.
- Other words may be used in the USA with exactly the same meaning as in the UK, but be spelt differently, for example, 'color', 'neighborhood'. *Note*: In this text, spellings have been changed to agree with UK usage.

The next day was Sunday and everybody figured that my mother would be sure to give in and ride in the Cadillac. After all, the family always went to church together on Sunday. But she didn't give in. What was worse she wouldn't let Wilma and me ride in the Cadillac either. She took us each by the hand, walked past the Cadillac where my father stood waiting and headed on towards the church, three blocks away. I was really mad at her now. I had been looking forward to driving up to the church in that gold Cadillac and having everybody see.

On most Sunday afternoons during the summertime, my mother, my father, Wilma, and I would go for a ride. Sometimes we just rode around the city and visited friends and family. Sometimes we made short trips over to Chicago or Peoria or Detroit to see relatives there or to Cleveland where we had relatives too, but we could also see the Cleveland Indians play. Sometimes we joined our aunts and uncles and drove in a caravan out to the park or to the beach. At the park or the beach Wilma and I would run and play. My mother and my aunts would spread a picnic and my father and my uncles would shine their cars.

But on this Sunday afternoon my mother refused to ride any-where. She told Wilma and me that we could go. So we left her alone in the big, empty house, and the family cars, led by the gold Cadillac, headed for the park. For a while I played and had a good time, but then I stopped playing and went to sit with my father. Despite his laughter he seemed sad to me. I think he was missing my mother as much as I was.

That evening my father took my mother to dinner down at the corner café. They walked. Wilma and I stayed at the house chasing fireflies in the back yard. My aunts and uncles sat in the yard and on the porch, talking and laughing about the day and watching us. It was a soft summer's evening, the kind that came every day and was expected. The smell of charcoal and of barbecue drifting from up the block, the sound of laughter and music and talk drifting from yard to yard were all a part of it. Soon one of my uncles joined Wilma and me in our chase of fireflies and when my mother and father came home we were at it still. My mother and father watched us for a while, while everybody else watched them to see if my father would take out the Cadillac and if my mother would slide in beside him to take a ride. But it soon became evident that the dinner had not changed my mother's mind. She still refused to ride in the Cadillac. I just couldn't understand her objection to it.

Though my mother didn't like the Cadillac, everybody else in the neighbourhood certainly did. That meant quite a few folks too, since we lived on a very busy block. On one corner was a grocery store, a cleaner's, and a gas station. Across the street was a beauty shop and a fish market, and down the street was a bar, another grocery store, the Dixie Theatre, the café, and a drugstore. There were always people strolling to or from one of these places and because our house was right in the middle of the block just about everybody had to pass our house and the gold Cadillac. Sometimes people took in the Cadillac as they walked, their heads turning for a longer look as they passed. Then there were people who just outright stopped and took a good look before continuing on their way. I was proud to say that car belonged to my family. I felt mighty important as people called to me as I ran down the street. "Ey, 'lois! How's that Cadillac, girl? Riding fine?' I told my mother how much everybody liked that car. She was not impressed and made no comment.

Since just about everybody on the block knew everybody else, most folks knew that my mother wouldn't ride in the Cadillac. Because of that, my father took a lot of good-natured kidding from the men. My mother got kidded too as the women said if she didn't ride in that car, maybe some other woman would. And everybody laughed about it and began to bet on who would give in first, my mother or my father. But then my father said he was going to drive the car south into Mississippi to visit my grandparents and everybody stopped laughing.

My uncles stopped.

So did my aunts.

Everybody.

'Look here, Wilbert,' said one of my uncles, 'it's too dangerous. It's like putting a loaded gun to your head.'

'I paid good money for that car,' said my father. 'That gives me a right to drive it where I please. Even down to Mississippi.'

My uncles argued with him and tried to talk him out of driving the car south. So did my aunts and so did the neighbours, Mr LeRoy, Mr Courtland and Mr Pondexter. They said it was a dangerous thing, a mighty dangerous thing, for a black man to drive an expensive car into the rural South.

'Not much those folks hate more'n to see a northern Negro coming down there in a fine car,' said Mr Pondexter. 'They see those Ohio licence plates, they'll figure you coming down uppity, trying to lord your fine car over them!'

I listened, but I didn't understand. I didn't understand why they didn't want my father to drive that car south. It was his.

'Listen to Pondexter, Wilbert!' cried another uncle. 'We might've fought a war to free people overseas, but we're not free here! Man, those white folks down south'll lynch you soon's look at you. You know that!'

Wilma and I looked at each other. Neither one of us knew what *lynch* meant, but the word sent a shiver through us. We held each other's hand.

My father was silent, then he said: 'All my life I've had to be heedful of what white folks thought. Well, I'm tired of that. I worked hard for everything I got. Got it honest, too. Now I got that Cadillac because I liked it and because it meant something to me that somebody like me from Mississippi could go and buy it. It's my car, I paid for it, and I'm driving it south.'

My mother, who had said nothing through all this, now stood. 'Then the girls and I'll be going too,' she said.

'No!' said my father.

My mother only looked at him and went off to the kitchen.

My father shook his head. It seemed he didn't want us to go. My uncles looked at each other, then at my father. 'You set on doing this, we'll all go,' they said. 'That way we can watch out for each other.' My father took a moment and nodded. Then my aunts got up and went off to their kitchens too.

A **dialect** is a version of a language which shows differences in grammar and vocabulary from **standard English**. Speakers of English who live in different regions of the UK, or in different countries where the national language is English (for example, the USA and Australia), may speak a dialect.

Reading for meaning

1 How does the writer convey mother's disapproval of the Cadillac?

2 In what ways does the atmosphere of the story suddenly change from good-humoured to threatening?

3 How does the writer show the closeness of the family when it senses danger? *Hint: Think about how they speak to each other, as well as what they do.*

4 Why does the family decide to drive south despite the known risks?

5 Why does mother agree to ride in the car, and to take the girls on the journey, after all?

All the next day my aunts and my mother cooked and the house was filled with delicious smells. They fried chicken and baked hams and cakes and sweet potato pies and mixed potato salad. They filled jugs with water and punch and coffee. Then they packed everything in huge picnic baskets along with bread and boiled eggs, oranges and apples, plates and napkins, spoons and forks and cups. They placed all that food on the back seats of the cars. It was like a grand, grand picnic we were going on, and Wilma and I were mighty excited. We could hardly wait to start.

My father, my mother, Wilma and I got into the Cadillac. My uncles, my aunts, my cousins got into the Ford, the Buick, and the Chevrolet, and we rolled off in our caravan headed south. Though my mother was finally riding in the Cadillac, she had no praise for it. In fact, she said nothing about it at all. She still seemed upset and since she still seemed to feel the same about the car, I wondered why she had insisted upon making this trip with my father.

We left the city of Toledo behind, drove through Bowling Green and down through the Ohio countryside of farms and small towns, through Dayton and Cincinnati, and across the Ohio River into Kentucky. On the other side of the river my father stopped the car and looked back at Wilma and me and said, 'Now from here on, whenever we stop and there're white people around, I don't want either one of you to say a word. *Not one word!* Your mother and I'll do all the talking. That understood?'

'Yes, sir,' Wilma and I both said, though we didn't truly understand why.

My father nodded, looked at my mother and started the car again. We rolled on, down Highway 25 and through the bluegrass hills of Kentucky. Soon we began to see signs. Signs that read: WHITE ONLY, COLOURED NOT ALLOWED. Hours later, we left the Bluegrass State and crossed into Tennessee. Now we saw even more of the signs saying: WHITE ONLY, COLOURED NOT ALLOWED. We saw the signs above water fountains and in restaurant windows. We saw them in ice-cream parlours and at

hamburger stands. We saw them in front of hotels and motels, and on the restroom doors of filling stations. I didn't like the signs. I felt as if I were in a foreign land.

I couldn't understand why the signs were there and I asked my father what the signs meant. He said they meant we couldn't drink from the water fountains. He said they meant we couldn't stop to sleep in the motels. He said they meant we couldn't stop to eat in the restaurants. I looked at the grand picnic basket I had been enjoying so much. Now I understood why my mother had packed it. Suddenly the picnic did not seem so grand.

Finally we reached Memphis. We got there at a bad time. Traffic was heavy and we got separated from the rest of the family. We tried to find them but it was no use. We had to go on alone. We reached the Mississippi state line and soon after we heard a police siren. A police car came up behind us. My father slowed the Cadillac, then stopped. Two white policemen got out of their car. They eyeballed the Cadillac and told my father to get out.

'Whose car is this, boy?' they asked.

I saw anger in my father's eyes. 'It's mine,' he said.

'You're a liar,' said one of the policemen. 'You stole this car.'

'Turn around, put your hands on top of that car and spread-eagle,' said the other policeman.

My father did as he was told. They searched him and I didn't understand why. I didn't understand either why they had called my father a liar and didn't believe that

the Cadillac was his. I wanted to ask but I remembered my father's warning not to say a word and I obeyed that warning.

The policemen told my father to get in the back of the police car. My father did. One policeman got back into the police car. The other policeman slid behind the wheel of our Cadillac. The police car started off. The Cadillac followed. Wilma and I looked at each other and at our mother. We didn't know what to think. We were scared.

The Cadillac followed the police car into a small town and stopped in front of the police station. The policeman stepped out of our Cadillac and took the keys. The other policeman took my father into the police station.

'Mother-Dear!' Wilma and I cried. 'What're they going to do to our daddy? They going to hurt him?'

'He'll be all right,' said my mother. 'He'll be all right.' But she didn't sound so sure of that. She seemed worried.

We waited. More than three hours we waited. Finally my father came out of the police station. We had lots of questions to ask him. He said the police had given him a ticket for speeding and locked him up. But then the judge had come. My father had paid the ticket and they had let him go.

He started the Cadillac and drove slowly out of the town, below the speed limit. The police car followed us. People standing on steps and sitting on porches and in front of stores stared at us as we passed. Finally we were out of the town. The police car still followed. Dusk was falling. The night grew black and finally the police car turned around and left us.

We drove and drove. But my father was tired now and my grand-parents' farm was still far away. My father said he had to get some sleep and since my mother didn't drive, he pulled into a grove of trees at the side of the road and stopped.

'I'll keep watch,' said my mother.

'Wake me if you see anybody,' said my father.

'Just rest,' said my mother.

So my father slept. But that bothered me. I needed him awake. I was afraid of the dark and of the woods and of whatever lurked there. My father was the one who kept us safe, he and my uncles. But already the police had taken my father away from us once today and my uncles were lost.

'Go to sleep, baby,' said my mother. 'Go to sleep.'

But I was afraid to sleep until my father woke. I had to help my mother keep watch. I figured I had to help protect us too, in case the police came back and tried to take my father away again. There was a long, sharp knife in the picnic basket and I took hold of it, clutching it tightly in my hand. Ready to strike, I sat there in the back of the car, eyes wide, searching the blackness outside the Cadillac. Wilma, for a while, searched the night too, then she fell asleep. I didn't want to sleep, but soon I found I couldn't help myself as an unwelcome drowsiness came over me. I had an uneasy sleep and when I woke it was dawn and my father was gently shaking me. I woke with a start and my hand went up, but the knife wasn't there. My mother had it.

My father took my hand. 'Why were you holding the knife, 'lois?' he asked.

I looked at him and at my mother. 'I – I was scared,' I said.

My father was thoughtful. 'No need to be scared now, sugar,' he said. 'Daddy's here and so is Mother-Dear.' Then after a glance at my mother, he got out of the car, walked to the road, looked down it one way, then the other. When he came back and started the motor, he turned the Cadillac north, not south.

'What're you doing?' asked my mother.

'Heading back to Memphis,' said my father. 'Cousin Halton's there. We'll leave the Cadillac and get his car. Driving this car any farther south with you and the girls in the car, it's just not worth the risk.'

Accent is how a speaker pronounces language. It varies according to the region or country the speaker comes from, and their social class or group. All spoken language is delivered with an accent, and writers sometimes use non-standard spellings to try to indicate how characters' words should be pronounced.

Reading for meaning

1 How does the writer help you understand the narrator's feeling that she is 'in a foreign land'?

2 Why do you sympathise with the family rather than the Mississippi police? *Hint: Think about how the police speak to the family as well as what they do.*

3 How is the sense of fear built up when the family continue their journey after the encounter with the police?

4 What do father's final words in this part of the text tell you about him?

5 What different kinds of courage are shown by the various family members when they were in Mississippi?

And so that's what we did. Instead of driving through Mississippi in golden splendour, we travelled its streets and roads and highways in Cousin Halton's solid, yet not so splendid, four-year-old Chevy. When we reached my grandparents' farm, my uncles and aunts were already there. Everybody was glad to see us. They had been worried. They asked about the Cadillac. My father told them what had happened, and they nodded and said he had done the best thing.

We stayed one week in Mississippi. During that week I often saw my father, looking deep in thought, walk off alone across the family land. I saw my mother watching him. One day I ran after my father, took his hand, and walked the land with him. I asked him all the questions that were on my mind. I asked him why the policemen had treated him the way they had and why people didn't want us to eat in the restaurants or drink from the water fountains or sleep in the hotels. I told him I just didn't understand all that.

My father looked at me and said that it all was a difficult thing to understand and he didn't really understand it himself. He said it all had to do with the fact that black people had once been forced to be slaves. He said it had to do with our skins being coloured. He said it had to do with stupidity and ignorance. He said it had to do with the law, the law that said we could be treated like this here in the South. And for that matter, he added, any other place in these United States where folks thought the same as so many folks did here in the South. But he also said, 'I'm hoping one day though we can drive that long road down here and there won't be any signs. I'm hoping one day the police won't stop us just because of the colour of our skins and we're riding in a gold Cadillac with northern plates.'

When the week ended, we said a sad good-bye to my grand-parents and all the Mississippi family and headed in a caravan back towards Memphis. In Memphis we returned Cousin Halton's car and got our Cadillac. Once we were home my father put the Cadillac in the garage and didn't drive it. I didn't hear my mother say any more about the Cadillac. I didn't hear my father speak of it either.

Some days passed and then on a bright Saturday afternoon while Wilma and I were playing in the back yard, I saw my father go into the garage. He opened the garage doors wide so the sunshine streamed in, and began to shine the Cadillac. I saw my mother at the kitchen window staring out across the yard at my father. For a long time, she stood there watching my father shine his car. Then she came out and crossed the yard to the garage and I heard her say, 'Wilbert, you keep the car.'

He looked at her as if he had not heard.

'You keep it,' she repeated and turned and walked back to the house.

My father watched her until the back door had shut behind her.

Then he went on shining the car and soon began to sing. About an hour later he got into the car and drove away. That evening when he came back he was walking. The Cadillac was nowhere in sight.

'Daddy, where's our new Cadillac?' I demanded to know. So did Wilma.

He smiled and put his hand on my head. 'Sold it,' he said as my mother came into the room.

'But how come?' I asked. 'We poor now?'

'No, sugar. We've got more money towards our new house now and we're all together. I figure that makes us about the richest folks in the world.' He smiled at my mother and she smiled too and came into his arms.

After that we drove around in an old 1930s Model A Ford my father had. He said he'd factory-ordered us another Mercury, this time with my mother's approval. Despite that, most folks on the block figured we had fallen on hard times after such a splashy showing of good times and some folks even laughed at us as the Ford rattled around the city. I must admit that at first I was pretty much embarrassed to be riding around in that old Ford after the splendour of the Cadillac. But my father said to hold my head high. We and the family knew the truth. As fine as the Cadillac had been, he said, it had pulled us apart for a while. Now, as ragged and noisy as that old Ford was, we all rode in it together and we were a family again. So I held my head high.

Still though, I often thought of that Cadillac. We had had the Cadillac only a little more than a month, but I wouldn't soon forget its splendour or how I'd felt riding around inside it. I wouldn't soon forget either the ride we had taken south in it. I wouldn't soon forget the signs, the policemen, or my fear. I would remember that ride and the gold Cadillac all my life.

Reading for meaning

1 Why has mother's attitude towards the gold Cadillac changed from what it was at the beginning of the story?

2 Why does father get rid of the car in the end?

3 What have the different members of the family learnt from the journey? How are they different now from what they were at the beginning of the story?

4 How would you describe the storyteller's feelings in the last paragraph? *Hint: Does she have mixed feelings about the car and the experience of travelling south in it?*

5 a) What subtitles would you give to each of the four sections of this story? Why?

   b) If you had to choose an incident from each section to illustrate, what would you choose, and why?

Vocabulary and spelling

1 a) What spelling rule does the plural 'wives' illustrate?
   b) What spelling rules do the plurals 'keys' and 'babies' illustrate?

   Make a note of these in your spelling book.

2 Apostrophes are used in 'The Gold Cadillac' for a number of purposes. Why are apostrophes needed in each of these examples?
   a) 'What 'bout you, 'lois?'
   b) Summer's evening
   c) 'Man, those white folks down south'll lynch you soon's look at you.'

3 In 'The Gold Cadillac', the word 'who's' is used. A **homonym** of 'who's' is 'whose'.
   a) What do these two words mean?
   b) Find two other words in the text for which you know a homonym, and explain what the difference in meaning is in each case

4 Look again at the second paragraph on page 91. In the last two sentences, what part of speech is the repeated word 'would', and what is its purpose in the meaning of those sentences?

5 In the second section of 'The Gold Cadillac', look again at the paragraph beginning 'Though my mother didn't like the Cadillac …'. Write down all the examples of **USA English**, both vocabulary and grammar, that you can find in this paragraph.

A **homonym** is a word with:

- the same spelling (in which case it is a **homograph**) *and/or*
- the same sound as another (in which case it is a **homophone**), but with a different meaning.

For example, 'calf' (meaning young cow or part of the leg) is a homograph and a homophone, and 'read/reed' is a homophone.

Sentences, paragraphs and punctuation

1 Towards the end of the third section of 'The Gold Cadillac', the text says 'my uncles were lost'. What different meanings might these words have?

2 Near the start of this story, the writer refers to 'the kitchen where my mother was cooking'. The last five words of this sentence form a **adverbial clause (of place)** which expands the noun 'kitchen'. Find two other examples of adverbial clauses in 'The Gold Cadillac'.

An **adverbial clause** adds to the meaning of the verb in the main clause of a sentence. Adverbial clauses may be clauses of:

- time (usually introduced by connectives such as 'when', 'after', 'before')
- place (introduced by 'where[ver]')
- reason (introduced by 'because', 'since', 'whereas')
- manner (introduced by 'how', 'as')
- comparison (introduced by 'than', 'as')
- purpose (introduced by 'so that', 'in case')
- result (introduced by 'so [that]')
- condition (introduced by 'if', 'unless')
- concession (introduced by '[al]though', 'even though').

3   What can you comment about the different grammatical structures of these sentences? For example, why has the writer used them and what effects do they achieve?

  a) 'Running down the hall, we banged on all the apartment doors.'

  b) 'Despite his laughter he seemed sad to me.'

  c) 'But none of us had had enough of the car so my father put the car on the road and we drove all the way to Detroit.'

4   Near the end of the third section of 'The Gold Cadillac', what meaning does the dash in the sentence: ' "I – I was scared," I said' convey to you?

Language variation

1   Look at these two quotations from 'The Gold Cadillac':

  ● 'Daddy say come on out and see this new car!'

  ● 'Well, what she say?'

How are the **verb** forms different from **standard English**? How many other non-standard verb forms can you find in the text?

2   In your group, carry out some research to find out about different varieties of English that are spoken throughout the world. Present a display of your findings, such as:

  ● places where English is the major language

  ● some of the grammatical differences in varieties of English

  ● the numbers of people who use different forms of English, etc.

As a group, prepare and deliver to the rest of the class a clear explanation of what you have researched, using your display as a visual aid.

Writing to imagine, explore and entertain

Write your own story about someone who learns or discovers something important as a result of a journey.

● Make sure that you entertain the reader by helping him or her to imagine the settings, characters and situations.

● Remember to explore what it is that the central character learns: this is more important than creating an action-packed narrative!

Writing to inform, explain and describe

Write a playscript in which two people describe and explain to each other the advantages and disadvantages of computers in modern life.

Both characters speak English, but in quite different ways.

- One is a teenager who uses both technical language (or 'jargon') and **slang.**

- The other is an elderly person who speaks **standard English** and does not know any specialist computer language.

Include stage directions, to show how each character tries to inform the other about his or her attitude towards information and communication technology. *Hint: If you are not sure about how to set out a playscript, look at an example (and remember the task on page 23).*

Drama

Prepare an improvised scene based on the following situation, which arises after the end of this story:

The narrator ('lois) is with some friends, who tease her about why her family does not have the Cadillac any more. She tries to explain the reasons.

You can decide:
- whether the friends understand her or not
- how they react towards her
- what she then does.

You can introduce other members of her family into the scene if you wish.

Review

What did you particularly enjoy in this chapter?

What did you not like very much?

Was there anything:

- you found difficult to understand?
- you discovered or understood for the first time?

Use this checklist to help you answer these questions and to review the progress you have made.

- **You have read**: a poem written about one hundred years ago; two recount texts; two holiday advertisements; a complete modern short story.

- **You have thought about how you respond to texts, and how writers use**: facts and opinions; descriptive and technical language; slang, contractions, dialect and accent; symbolism; layout and presentational features; different text types such as recount and myth.

- **You have written to**: imagine, explore and entertain – some diary entries, a story and a playscript; inform, explain and describe – about a place; persuade, argue and advise – an advertisement; analyse, review and comment – a response to a numerical table.

- **To improve your writing you have thought about**: purpose and audience; sentence structures, including adverbial clauses; aspects of spelling such as homonyms and plurals; apostrophes, and other punctuation.

- **Your speaking and listening work has included**: discussing texts in pairs and as a group; reporting back to the class; devising and performing improvised drama; evaluating your own and others' work.

- **You may have used ICT to**: research, organise and present a vocabulary list; create an advertisement; research and produce visual aids; spellcheck, and present final drafts of your writing neatly and attractively.

3 Mysteries

Most of us enjoy a good mystery story and being scared – as long as we can decide when to stop, by closing the book, shutting our eyes or switching off the television! Many **fairy stories**, **legends** and other **traditional tales** involve scary situations – strange and terrifying monsters, witchcraft and magic, for example.

Modern writers and film-makers often use similar elements to jangle the nerves of their readers and viewers.

3.1 Traditional tales

The Fisherman

This short story was written at the end of the nineteenth century by the Norwegian, Jonas Lie, but it is like a fairy story or traditional tale in many ways. Before you read it, discuss the following questions, first with a partner and then as a class.

Before you read

1 What sorts of people appear in legends, fairy stories and traditional tales? *Hint: Can you put them into different groups or categories?*

2 What sorts of situation and event often occur in such narratives? *Hint: Think of examples from your previous reading.*

3 Why do you think people still listen to stories like that? *Hint: Think of stories that you particularly remember – why is that?*

As you read

Think about:

- how it is *like* a traditional tale, legend or fairy story

- how it is *different* from those kinds of stories

- what the writer's purpose is in writing this story.

- **Fairy stories** are based on traditional tales and contain magical people and situations. The plots may be quite gruesome and frightening.
- **Legends** are usually about well-known actual people, such as St George. The stories may include true events, but they may have been added to over the years to make it seem more exciting or heroic.
- Other kinds of **traditional tale** may involve ordinary people who perform extraordinary deeds, for example Isak in 'The Fisherman'. Both legends and traditional tales are meant to suggest a moral, or message, to the reader.

The Fisherman

There was a young fisherman from Helgeland whose name was Isak.

One day he was out in the fjord fishing for halibut when he felt something heavy on his line. He reeled it in and discovered that he had caught a fisherman's boot. 'Strange,' he said, staring at his catch. The boot looked just like the type his brother was wearing when he was lost in the fjord during a terrible storm. There was something in the boot but he did not dare look what it was.

And he did not know what to do with his gruesome find.

He could not take it home. It would scare the living daylights out of his mother. But he could not bring himself to throw it back.

He decided to take the boot to the local vicar and ask him to give it a proper burial.

'I can't bury a fisherman's boot,' said the vicar.

'No, I suppose not.'

But Isak wanted to know how much of a person there had to be before it could have a proper burial.

'I don't know the answer,' said the vicar. 'It's not a tooth or a finger or a lock of hair. However, there should be enough left for me to know that it once had a soul. And a toenail at the bottom of a boot is, quite frankly, too little.

Despite the vicar's ruling, Isak decided to bury the boot in the graveyard anyway. He did it discreetly, then left. He felt he had done the best he could. Surely it was better to place something belonging to his dead brother in hallowed ground than to throw the boot back out to sea?

It was late autumn when he was out after cod and brought up a leather belt. He recognised it immediately: it was his brother's.

The buckle had been tarnished by the sea. He remembered quite clearly how his brother had fashioned the leather, which they had got from their old horse when it had died. They had brought the buckle together over at a general stores one Saturday. They had had a bit to drink and had flirted with the girls who made the sails down by the quay.

He kept quiet about the belt and hid it in his room. He did not want to cause his mother any pain by telling her about it.

As the winter drew on he began to think more and more about what the vicar had said.

He began to worry about how he would react if he reeled in another boot or some bone that the fish had been gnawing at.

And so he became scared of going to fish in the fjord. Yet he could not stop himself going back to the places where he had found his brother's remains. He desperately wanted to find enough of his brother so that the vicar could tell that the soul had been there; then the vicar could perform the ceremony.

And then he began to have nightmares.

The door would fly open in the middle of the night and a cold wind stinking of seaweed would blow in and he sensed his brother was in the room, moaning and screaming in pain, howling for his lost foot. Being without it was agony.

Isak could hardly work now. He could barely lift a hand; he just stared into the middle distance. He felt that the burden of burying his brother's boot in the cemetery was finally driving him crazy.

Yet he could not throw the boot back in the water.

All he wanted was for his brother to get a decent burial. He could not bear the thought of his corpse lying out there at the bottom of the fjord being messed about by whatever was down there.

Finally he plucked up the courage to start fishing again. At first he fished close in to the land but he did not have much success. So he took his boat further out to try his luck there.

It was early evening and he was preparing his first cast. He got hold of the lead weight and threw it into the water. The line with the fifty baited hooks fairly flew after it but the last hook caught his eye as it went past, tore the eyeball from the socket and down it went to the bottom of the fjord.

There was no point in looking for it; so he rowed back home.

That night he lay in bed, a bandage over his eye. He was in great pain and could not sleep. Everything seemed to go black and he thought he must be the most forlorn person in the world.

Then a strange event occurred: he felt as if he was transported to the bottom of the sea. As he looked round, he noticed how the fish flitted about near the baited hooks. When they took the bait, they struggled like mad to be free: first a cod, next a haddock. Then a small shark appeared, looked closely at the bait, and took it. While all this was going on, Isak realised what he had really been looking at: it was the remains of a body; he could see the leather-clad back quite clearly; it was jammed under a five-pronged anchor.

As he was staring at what was left of his brother, a large fish approached the bait. Then everything went dark.

'You must let me go in the morning,' said the large fish. 'The hook is agony, agony. By the way, only fish at night when the tide is on the turn – it's the only time you'll catch anything.'

Next day Isak went down to the cemetery and picked up a piece of broken gravestone to use as a weight for his fishing line. That evening as the tide turned, he set his line.

Straight away he got a bite and hauled in the line: there was the five pronged anchor with the leather coat on it. Looking more closely, he saw the remains of an arm in the sleeve. That was all; the fish had obviously had the rest.

He took his grim catch to the vicar.

'You really expect me to give the last rites to a sodden old bit of leather?'

'Don't forget the boot as well.'

'Flotsam and jetsam is not enough,' thundered the vicar.

Isak looked the vicar straight in the eye. 'The burden of my brother's boot has been hard enough to bear. I can't face the arm as well.'

'And I am not prepared to waste a patch of hallowed ground on a load of rubbish!' Now the vicar was angry.

'No, I suppose not.' And with that Isak went home.

He could not relax. The weight of his dead brother preyed on his mind. At night he saw that same big fish swimming sadly round in the same slow circle. It was almost as though there was an invisible net surrounding it. And he stared and stared at it until his blind eye ached with the pain. Then a large octopus drenched everything with foul, dark ink; and darkness descended.

One evening he went out in his boat and let the current take it out towards a group of little islands. There the boat came to a standstill and everything became quiet. Not a sound was to be heard. All of a sudden a huge bubble burst by the side of the boat.

Isak saw something and he understood what it meant.

'The vicar will be carrying out a funeral soon,' he said to himself.

From that moment on, Isak got a reputation for having psychic powers. He could predict where the best places to fish would be, and, when people asked him how he knew, he replied, 'It's my brother who gives me the information.'

And then came the day when the vicar had to go out into the fjord to do his annual blessing of the water. Isak was one of the men who rowed the vicar out into the fjord. In the distance there was a rumble of thunder as the vicar completed his thanksgiving.

'The weather looks as if it's on the turn,' said the vicar. 'Best we get back.'

Just as they started on the return journey, a storm hit them. The snow swirled about and the sea seemed as big as houses. Then one of the timbers cracked and water poured into the boat and everyone screamed that they were going to sink.

'Be calm. We'll make it,' said Isak grimly as he held fast to the rudder.

The moon broke through the cloud cover and shone on the hole in the boat. A strange figure was there, baling out the water for all he was worth.

'Who's that man?' said the vicar. 'I don't understand. He's baling out water with a fisherman's boot. His legs are bare and … his leather jacket seems empty.'

'You've seen him before,' said Isak.

At this the vicar lost his patience. 'I command you by the hand of God to leave this boat, unholy spirit.'

'Fine,' said Isak, 'but can you command the water to stop pouring in through that hole?'

The vicar paused. 'The man does seem to have superhuman power and at this moment we do have great need of such a man. It is no crime to help one of God's servants across a stormy sea. So, what do you require in return for saving us?'

The wind howled.

'Just a few shovels full of earth placed on a sailor's boot and a leather sleeve,' said Isak.

'I grant you your blessing. You'll get your proper burial.'

No sooner had the vicar uttered these words than a huge wave seemed to pick the vicar's boat up and shoot it towards dry land, where it came to rest with a thud, breaking the mast clean in two.

Reading for meaning

1 How much do you find out about Isak and his family from the first four paragraphs?

2 What sort of a person is the vicar? *Hint: Look at his words and what he does. Does he change at all?*

3 Which features of this story make it like a traditional tale?

4 Which features of this story are unlike a traditional tale?

5 Why do you think the mast of the boat breaks in two at the very end of the story?

6 What is the moral, or message, of the story?

Vocabulary and spelling

1 Find all the words in this story which are to do with fishing and the sea. Make an alphabetical list of them and write the meaning of each word beside it.

2 Find out the meanings of these words, and where each of them comes from:
   a) hallowed
   b) corpse
   c) transported
   d) rites
   e) psychic.

On the worksheet, write the meaning and origin of each word, and any similar words you know or can discover. *Hint: Use a dictionary – an* **etymological** *dictionary is useful if you can find one.*

Explain the spelling rule these words illustrate, and give another example of a word family which follows the rule:
bury–burying–burial–buried.

Sentences, paragraphs and punctuation

1   Look again at the paragraph on page 111 which begins 'The buckle had been tarnished by the sea.' This sentence is in the **passive** voice.

　　a)　Rewrite the sentence in the **active** voice.

　　b)　Why do you think the writer chose to use the passive voice here? *Hint: What is the most important word in the sentence?*

2   In the same paragraph, look at the **tenses** of the verbs. One is in the **simple past** tense ('remembered'), but others are in the **past perfect tense**, which uses the verb 'had' in front of the **simple past** form ('fashioned', 'got', 'died', 'bought', 'had', 'flirted'). Why are different tenses needed to tell this part of the story?

3   Look again at the paragraph on page 112 beginning 'Then a strange event occurred …'. Using the worksheet, explain how the writer uses punctuation to make the meaning clear.

Verb tenses tell us when something happens.

* The **simple past tense** describes something that has already happened, for example 'I ran away'.
* The **simple present tense** describes something that is happening now, for example 'I run away'.
* The **present continuous tense** describes something that is ongoing, for example 'I am running away'.
* The **future tense** describes something that will or may happen, for example 'I will run away'.
* The **present perfect tense** describes a situation in the past looked at from the present, for example 'I have run away'.
* The **past perfect tense** refers to a situation in the past that came about before another situation in the past, for example 'I had run away'.

Drama

'The Fisherman' is a story which could be dramatised in different ways. One way would be as a radio play with a narrator reading most of the story, and actors reading the words spoken by Isak, the vicar and the large fish.

1 In groups, prepare a dramatised reading, as if you were doing it for the radio, of the text from 'From that moment on, …' to the end.

   Each group will need at least one narrator, someone to be Isak, someone to be the vicar and at least one other person to supply the sound effects.

   When you are planning your reading, look at the places in the story where someone speaks. Think about:

   ● how could you make it clear who is speaking

   ● whether you want the narrator to speak the phrases used in the text such as 'he said'. What difference would it make if you left these phrases out?

   ● whether you want to use more than one narrator. What would be the advantages and disadvantages of this?

   When you perform your reading, the audience won't be able to see you so you need to speak clearly.

2 Listen to the performances of the other groups.

   Think about:

   ● whether the words are spoken clearly and at the right speed

   ● whether it is easy to tell the difference between the voices

   ● whether you feel the characters' emotions through the expression in the voices

   ● whether the sound effects create an appropriate atmosphere

   ● how the performances are different – which one works best and why.

A Midsummer Night's Dream

This is an extract from Shakespeare's *A Midsummer Night's Dream*. Like 'The Fisherman', this play contains elements of a **fairy story** – in fact, a number of the characters are fairies!

One of Shakespeare's best-known characters appears in this play – Puck, or Robin Goodfellow as he was sometimes called. Puck was a legendary spirit with a mischievous nature. In Shakespearian times, some superstitious people used to put out a bowl of milk for Puck at night, to keep him happy and prevent him doing any mischief in or around their homes.

In this conversation between Puck and a fairy, you hear the sort of things Puck used to get up to: in a modern text, he might appear as a poltergeist with a sense of humour!

A Midsummer Night's Dream
Act 2, Scene 1

FAIRY Either I mistake your shape and making quite,
       Or else you are that shrewd and knavish sprite
       Called Robin Goodfellow. Are not you he
       That frights the maidens of the villagery,   35
       Skim milk, and sometimes labour in the quern,
       And bootless make the breathless housewife churn,
       And sometime make the drink to bear no barm,
       Mislead night-wanderers, laughing at their harm?
       Those that 'Hobgoblin' call you, and 'Sweet Puck' 40
       You do their work, and they shall have good luck.
       Are not you he?
PUCK   Thou speakest aright;
       I am that merry wanderer of the night.
       I jest to Oberon, and make him smile
       When I a fat and bean-fed horse beguile,   45
       Neighing in likeness of a filly foal;
       And sometime lurk I in a gossip's bowl
       In very likeness of a roasted crab,
       And when she drinks, against her lips I bob,
       And on her withered dewlap pour the ale.   50
       The wisest aunt, telling the saddest tale,
       Sometime for threefoot stool mistaketh me;
       Then slip I from her bum, down topples she,
       And 'Tailor' cries, and falls into a cough;
       And then the whole choir hold their hips and loffe, 55
       And waxen in their mirth, and neeze, and swear
       A merrier hour was never wasted there.

Shakespeare's language

1 When the fairy calls Puck 'shrewd', this word could mean either 'evil' or 'mischievous' in Shakespearian times. Which adjective describes him better?

2 Some words in this text are no longer used in modern English, for example, 'quern', 'bootless', 'barm', 'waxen' and 'neeze'. Find out what these words mean, and what their modern equivalents might be.

3 Some words in this text have a slightly different form from the modern equivalent, for example, 'villagery' and 'loffe'. Why do you think Shakespeare used these forms? *Hint: Look at the ending of the previous line in both cases!*

4 What personal pronouns and **verb** endings can you find which are different from modern usage? Where are there also examples of modern pronouns and endings?

What does this suggest to you about changes that were taking place in the English language in Shakespeare's time?

5 Draw up a table like the one below and use it to list the words in this extract which are no longer used today or which have changed in meaning. Start with the words mentioned in the questions above, and then see if you can find any others in the extract.

Title of play	Language no longer used		Changed language		
	Word	Meaning	Word	Shakespearian meaning	Modern meaning

You can add to this table as you read other extracts from Shakespeare's plays.

Writing to inform, explain and describe

Compare your answers to question 4 in the 'Shakespeare's language' section opposite with others in your group.

Then check your ideas by carrying out some research about changes in the English language since Shakespeare's time

Plan and write a short account of what this extract from *A Midsummer Night's Dream* shows about changes in the English language since Shakespeare's time.

Speaking and listening

Think of things that frighten you, or frightened you when you were younger – things your friends or adults may have talked about, characters in books, or on television. Swap your experiences for a few minutes, and decide which is the most interesting. Work out how, as a group, you can tell the rest of the class about this in a vivid and exciting way.

Classic fiction

The Appointed Time

Charles Dickens is famous for the vivid detail in his novels. This detail gives life to his characters and his settings so that most readers find them convincing – even if the situations are unlikely to happen in real life. This extract is from *Bleak House*. It is the story of a long-running legal case, with many subplots.

In this extract, Tony Weevle and Mr Guppy are trying to get hold of some letters. The letters are in the hands of Mr Krook, who has a shop down-stairs in the house where Weevle lodges. They are waiting for midnight to strike – the 'appointed time' for Weevle to call on Krook.

Before you read

1 Dickens wrote this book between 1852 and 1853. The English language has changed in many ways since then. While you are reading the extract, look out for:

   ● unfamiliar words and expressions

   ● grammatical structures that seem unusual.

   Make a note of them to discuss before you do any work on the text.

2 Even if you do not understand every word, try to imagine the experience the two men are going through. Think about:

   ● how Dickens creates tension while Weevle and Guppy are waiting for the clock to strike

   ● how he increases the tension when they enter Krook's room

   ● how Dickens creates a sense of panic at the end of the extract

   ● what Weevle and Guppy have discovered.

The Appointed Time

Mr. Weevle, by stirring the fire suddenly, makes Mr. Guppy start as if his heart had been stirred instead.

'Fah! Here's more of this hateful soot hanging about,' says he. 'Let us open the window a bit and get a mouthful of air. It's too close.'

He raises the sash, and they both rest on the window-sill, half in and half out of the room. The neighbouring houses are too near to admit of their seeing any sky without craning their necks and looking up, but lights in frowsy windows here and there, and the rolling of distant carriages, and the new expression that there is of the stir of men, they find to be comfortable. ...

Mr. Guppy sitting on the window-sill, continues thoughtfully to tap it, and clasp it, and measure it with his hand, until he hastily draws his hand away.

'What, in the devil's name,' he says, 'is this! Look my fingers!'

A thick, yellow liquor defiles them, which is offensive to the touch and sight and more offensive to the smell. A stagnant, sickening oil with some natural repulsion in it that makes them both shudder.

'What have you been doing here? What have you been pouring out of window?'

'I pouring out of window! Nothing, I swear! Never, since I have been here!' cries the lodger.

And yet look here – and look here! When he brings the candle here, from the corner of the window-sill, it slowly drips and creeps away down the bricks, here lies in a little thick nauseous pool.

'This is a horrible house,' says Mr. Guppy, shutting down the window. 'Give me some water or I shall cut my hand off.'

He so washes, and rubs, and scrubs, and smells, and washes, that he has not long restored himself with a glass

of brandy and stood silently before the fire when Saint Paul's bell strikes twelve and all those other bells strike twelve from their towers of various heights in the dark air, and in their many tones. When all is quiet again, the lodger says, 'It's the appointed time at last. Shall I go?'

Mr. Guppy nods and gives him a 'lucky touch' on the back, but not with the washed hand, though it is his right hand.

He goes downstairs, and Mr. Guppy tries to compose himself before the fire for waiting a long time. But in no more than a minute or two the stairs creak and Tony comes swiftly back.

'Have you got them?'

'Got them! No. The old man's not there.'

He has been so horribly frightened in the short interval that his terror seizes the other, who makes a rush at him and asks loudly, 'What's the matter?'

'I couldn't make him hear, and I softly opened the door and looked in. And the burning smell is there – and the soot is there, and the oil is there – and he is not there!' Tony ends this with a groan.

Mr. Guppy takes the light. They go down, more dead than alive, and holding one another, push open the door of the back shop. The cat has retreated close to it and stands snarling, not at them, at something on the ground before the fire. There is a very little fire left in the grate, but there is a smouldering, suffocating vapour in the room and a dark, greasy coating on the walls and ceiling. The chairs and table, and the bottle so rarely absent from the table, all stand as usual. On one chair-back hang the old man's hairy cap and coat.

'Look!' whispers the lodger, pointing his friend's attention to these objects with a trembling finger. 'I told you so. When I saw him last, he took his cap off, took out the little bundle of old letters, hung his cap on the back of the chair – his coat was there already, for he had pulled that off before he went to put the shutters up – and I left him turning the letters over in his hand, standing just where that crumbled black thing is upon the floor.'

Is he hanging somewhere? They look up. No.

'See!' whispers Tony. 'At the foot of the same chair there lies a dirty bit of thin red cord that they tie up pens with. That went round the letters. He undid it slowly, leering and laughing at me, before he began to turn them over, and threw it there. I saw it fall.'

'What's the matter with the cat?' says Mr. Guppy. 'Look at her!'

'Mad, I think. And no wonder in this evil place.'

They advance slowly, looking at all these things. The cat remains where they found her, still snarling at the something on the ground before the fire and between the two chairs. What is it? Hold up the light.

Here is a small burnt patch of flooring; here is the tinder from a little bundle of burnt paper, but not so light as usual, seeming to be steeped in something; and here is – is it the cinder of a small charred and broken log of wood sprinkled with white ashes, or is it coal? Oh, horror, he *is* here! And this from which we run away, striking out the light and overturning one another into the street, is all that represents him.

Help, help, help! Come into this house for heaven's sake!

Plenty will come in, but none can help. … Call the death by any name you will, attribute it to whom you will, or say it might have been prevented how you will it is the same death eternally – inborn, inbred, engendered in the corrupted humours of the vicious body itself, and that only – spontaneous combustion, and none other of all the deaths that can be died.

Reading for meaning

1   Mr Guppy is always referred to by the writer as Mr Guppy; Mr Weevle, after the first mention of his name, is referred to as Tony. What does this make you feel about the two men?

2   Find places in this text where the writer seems to be speaking directly to you. What effect does this have? *Hint: How do you feel at these points?*

3   Why does Mr Guppy use his 'wrong' hand to give Tony Weevle a 'lucky touch'?

4   Why do you think Dickens has included a cat in this scene?

5   What do the two men see on the floor between the two chairs which terrifies them?

Authorial viewpoint When you read a text, how conscious are you of the author?

- If the story is written in the **first person**, that is 'I did so and so …', it seems as if the author and the storyteller are the same – but are they? If the storyteller is a murderer or a thief, does that mean the author shares the character's views? Probably not! The text may be written so it appears as if the character is telling his or her own story.

- Many texts are written in the **third person**, that is 'She did so and so …'. In these texts, it seems as though the author has total knowledge of all the characters, and so authorial viewpoint may seem to be more obvious. Sometimes, as in the extract from *Bleak House*, the author seems to step out of the story and speak directly to you in order to comment on a situation or a character.

When you read a text, think about the ideas the author is putting across to you, and how this is done. For example, what do you think Dickens' own thoughts about spontaneous combustion are? What makes you think this?

Vocabulary and spelling

1   What does the **simile** in the opening line of the text suggest about Mr Guppy's state of mind?

2   Reread the text from 'A thick, yellow liquor …' to '… nauseous pool'. What effect do the adjectives have in these lines? Why are some words repeated?

3   Why does the writer use so many **verbs** in the sentence 'He so washes, and rubs, and scrubs, and smells, and washes …'? What makes this description so effective?

4   What spelling rules about word endings are illustrated by the following words in the text:
   a) stirring?   d) hastily?
   b) hateful?   e) horribly?
   c) craning?

Sentences, paragraphs and punctuation

I   What effect does the **present tense** have in this extract?

2   When Weevle answers Guppy's question, 'What's the matter?', his reply repeats the word 'and' several times. What effect does this have? How does the punctuation help you read this in a particular way?

3   In the three paragraphs near the end, from 'They advance slowly …' to '…for heaven's sake!', Dickens does not punctuate any of the words as direct speech, although it sounds as though some of them are spoken (for example, 'What is it?, Oh, horror …, Help, help, help!'). Why do you think he left them unpunctuated?

4   The last sentence of this text is long and complicated. Rewrite it, using simpler vocabulary and splitting it into several sentences. Why do you think Dickens chose to write it in the way he did? Is your version easier to understand? Would it make an equally good ending?

Writing to imagine, explore and entertain

Write three paragraphs entitled 'The Discovery'. You are not going to write a complete story, but only the part where (as in the Dickens text) someone makes a dramatic discovery – just enough to whet the reader's appetite!

Your challenge is to make the reader of your **narrative** feel tension and excitement as you build up to the surprise at the end. Your surprise might be the discovery of something awful, or it might be something unexpectedly pleasant or amusing. Use the planning sheet to help you.

Murder and detective genre

Stories about murders – real or imagined – have been extremely popular for a very long time. Murders occur in some of the oldest surviving literature from around the world, and the detective story became one of the most popular **genres** during the last part of the nineteenth century, and ever since. Almost everyone has heard of Sherlock Holmes, Hercule Poirot, Inspector Morse and other fictional detectives. Books about actual murders – especially unsolved mysteries – continue to sell in large numbers.

Genre describes different types of writing with their own characteristics or features, for example crime writing, historical novels.

Crime writing

1 Why do you think people enjoy reading about crime and murder so much?

2 Describe a murder story or film which made a deep impression on you. What was memorable about it? *Hint: Think about the plot, the characters and the setting.*

3 What do you think are some of the main features of the detective story genre? *Hint: What would include if you were writing a detective story? How could you structure the story to keep readers interested?*

The Ballad of Charlotte Dymond

The first text you will read is based on a real murder, but it is not written as a non-fiction recount: it is written in the form of a modern **ballad**. The writer, Charles Causley, is a Cornishman who bases much of his work on local history. He likes to use traditional forms, such as the ballad, in his writing.

A **ballad** is a poem, sometimes set to music as a song, which tells a story.
- The stanzas are usually quite short, with a simple **rhythm** and **rhyme** scheme.
- There may be a lot of repetition, for example, of words or phrases, or even of a whole stanza which is used as a chorus or to remind you of the subject of the poem.
- Many ballads, like 'The Ballad of Charlotte Dymond', are based on actual events and people, although there are often imaginative additions or changes to the original details.

THE BALLAD OF CHARLOTTE DYMOND

Charlotte Dymond, a domestic servant aged eighteen, was
murdered near Rowtor Ford on Bodmin Moor on Sunday
14 April 1844, by her young man, a crippled farm-hand,
Matthew Weeks, aged twenty-two. A stone marks the spot.

It was a Sunday evening
   And in the April rain
That Charlotte went from our house
   And never came home again.

Her shawl of diamond redcloth,   5
   She wore a yellow gown,
She carried the green gauze handkerchief
   She bought in Bodmin town.

About her throat her necklace
   And in her purse her pay: 10
The four silver shillings
   She had at Lady Day.

In her purse four shillings
   And in her purse her pride
As she walked out one evening   15
   Her lover at her side.

Out beyond the marshes
   Where the cattle stand,
With her crippled lover
   Limping at her hand.   20

Charlotte walked with Matthew
   Through the Sunday mist,
Never saw the razor
   Waiting at his wrist.

Charlotte she was gentle   25
   But they found her in the flood
Her Sunday beads among the reeds
   Beaming with her blood.

Matthew, where is Charlotte,
   And wherefore has she flown?   30
For you walked out together
   And now are come alone.

Why do you not answer,
   Stand silent as a tree,
Your Sunday worsted stockings   35
   All muddied to the knee?

Why do you mend your breast-pleat
   With a rusty needle's thread
And fall with fears and silent tears
   Upon your single bed?   40

Why do you sit so sadly
   Your face the colour of clay
And with a green gauze handkerchief
   Wipe the sour sweat away?

Has she gone to Blisland   45
   To seek an easier place,
And is that why your eye won't dry
   And blinds your bleaching face?

'Take me home!' cried Charlotte,
   'I lie here in the pit!   50
A red rock rests upon my breasts
   And my naked neck is split!'

Her skin was soft as sable,
   Her eyes were wide as day,
Her hair was blacker than the bog   55
   That licked her life away.

Her cheeks were made of honey,
   Her throat was made of flame
Where all around the razor
   Had written its red name.   60

As Matthew turned at Plymouth
   About the tilting Hoe,
The cold and cunning Constable
   Up to him did go:

'I've come to take you, Matthew,   65
   Unto the Magistrate's door.
Come quiet now, you pretty poor boy,
   And you must know what for.'

'She is as pure,' cried Matthew,
   'As the early dew,   70
Her only stain it is the pain
   That round her neck I drew!

'She is as guiltless as the day
    She sprang forth from her mother.
The only sin upon her skin   75
    Is that she loved another.'

They took him off to Bodmin,
    They pulled the prison bell,
They sent him smartly up to Heaven
    And dropped him down to Hell.   80

All through the granite kingdom
    And on its travelling airs
Ask which of these two lovers
    The most deserves your prayers.

And your steel heart search, Stranger,   85
    That you may pause and pray
For lovers who come not to bed
    Upon their wedding day,

But lie upon the moorland
    Where stands the sacred snow   90
Above the breathing river,
    And the salt sea-winds go.

Reading for meaning

1 Why do you think the writer has included the details of the story he is about to tell at the start of the poem?

2 What details does the writer include to make the ballad seem like a true account of a real event? *Hint: Think about the setting – both geographical and historical – and the use of description and speech.*

3 Who is speaking this poem, do you think? Does the person change at any point? What effect does this have? *Hint: Compare the beginning with the section which starts at stanza 8, and the last three stanzas.*

4 What do you think the third stanza from the end means? What is your answer to the question it asks, and why?

5 What sticks in your mind when you have read this poem? Why?

6 Why do you think the writer chose to tell the story as a ballad?

Ballads

1 One common feature of ballads is the use of **archaic** words and phrases. Find some examples in this text, and explain:

● why you think the writer has used them

● what effects they achieve.

> **Archaic** forms of language – for example, vocabulary such as 'ere' (meaning 'before') or grammatical constructions such as 'thou knowest' instead of 'you know' – are often used by writers to create a sense of the past in a text set in a previous age.

2 In the third line of some stanzas of this text the writer uses **internal rhyme**. Why do you think he does this on these occasions?

> **Internal rhyme** describes the placing of two (or more) words which rhyme in the same line of a poem, for example 'Her Sunday beads among the reeds'.

3 Charles Causley uses **personification** several times. What effect does each use of personification have on the meaning and effect of the poem?

4 Repetition is another common feature of ballads. Find examples of repetition in this text. What different purposes and effects do they achieve?

Speaking and listening

Prepare a dramatic reading of 'The Ballad of Charlotte Dymond'. You will need to decide:

- how many separate characters you need

- the sort of voice each character requires

- how many different voices to use for the narrator

- how you will make the text seem dramatic to listeners.

When you have given your own performance and have listened to performances given by the other groups, discuss:

- which aspects of each performance were most effective, and why

- how you felt your own performance measured up against the others – its strengths and its weaknesses – and why.

Writing to explore, imagine and entertain

You are going to write your own ballad based on a real event. You need to choose this event carefully: it should be something dramatic with a strong (but not too complicated!) storyline.

You might choose:

- something which has happened to you – an accident, for example

- a historical event from recent times – for example, your favourite sports team or individual winning a competition

- a historical event from the past – for example, a famous battle.

When you have chosen the event, start to jot down:

- an outline of the events you will include, so that you can choose and sequence what is most important

135

- words and phrases which you might use, thinking about rhyming possibilities

- ideas about the stanza form, that is, the rhythm and rhyme scheme you will use.

  Hint: Stick to something simple, like the form used by Charles Causley in the text you have read: 4-line stanzas, with 6–8 'beats' in a line, and only two rhyming lines per stanza.

Now write your ballad, remembering to draft and revise where necessary – use your teacher and other pupils to advise you.

In previous centuries, before the age of television and the popular press, ballads were often sold in the streets in decorative printed versions with illustrations. You could decorate and illustrate your ballad for a class display.

Writing to persuade, argue and advise

Imagine you are Charlotte. Write what you say to Matthew to try to change his mind at the moment you realise he is going to harm you.

or

Imagine you are Matthew. Write what you say in court to try to pursuade the judge not to hang you for Charlotte's murder.

LONG-SONG SELLER.
"Two under fifty for a fardy'!"

The Casebook for Forensic Detection

Matthew, the murderer of Charlotte Dymond, was apparently caught without too much trouble. But sometimes it can be a long and difficult job to track down a murderer and prove his or her guilt. Advances in science have made this easier, and murderers may now be trapped by the smallest trace of themselves or of the weapons they leave behind at a murder scene. Even so, luck may still play a part, particularly in giving the police a lead as to who the criminal might be.

The next text is an extract from *The Casebook of Forensic Detection*. It describes one of the first times when ballistics evidence (evidence about guns and bullets) helped to convict two particularly vicious criminals. However, the police were first alerted to them by a suspect in an entirely different case.

BROWNE AND KENNEDY

In the years following World War I, America took a decisive lead in the fledgling science of firearms analysis. Europe's desultory progress was explained, in large measure, by the relative scarcity of guns on the street, but it was also due in part to a belief that armed gunmen were exclusively an American phenomenon, one most unlikely to cross the Atlantic. Such smug complacency was shattered by the events of September 26th, 1927.

On that night, two petty crooks, Frederick Browne, forty-six, and William Kennedy, thirty-six, set out from London by train to Billericay in Essex. Their intention was to steal a particular car that Browne had earmarked earlier. Thwarted in that desire – a barking dog scared them off – they broke into a garage belonging to a Dr. Edward Lovell, stole his blue Morris Cowley, and sped erratically back to London.

Some miles along a remote country lane, their haphazard progress drew the attention of Police Constable George Gutteridge, who flagged the Morris to a halt. He approached the car, shone his lamp on both men, and asked where they were going. Nettled by Browne's superciliousness Gutteridge reached for his notebook. As he did so, Browne drew a gun and fired twice. Gutteridge fell to the ground. Browne sprang from the car and stood over him. Perhaps mindful of the superstition that a murder victim's eyes record the last image they see, he leaned over the prostrate officer and shot out his eyes. Later that night, the two killers ditched the car in south London before catching a train to Browne's Golden Globe Garage in Battersea.

First light saw a fast-moving chain of events: A motorist found Constable Gutteridge's bullet riddled body lying beside the road, Dr. Lovell contacted the police to report the theft of his car, and the Morris was discovered in London. Investigators soon linked the three incidents.

The stolen car provided several promising clues. There were splashes of blood on the floor and running board, and under the passenger seat lay an empty cartridge case. This was handed to Robert Churchill for analysis. Churchill came from a family of London gunsmiths that made and sold sporting guns and rifles, but his real interest lay in the study of weapons and their projectiles. On those rare occasions when Scotland Yard needed to consult a firearms expert, his was the opinion in demand. He identified the cartridge as a Mark IV, an obsolete bullet filled with black

powder and manufactured at the Woolwich Arsenal in 1914. On its base he noted a tiny raised imperfection, the result of a faulty breech block on the gun that had fired it. Churchill said that the murder weapon was almost certainly a .455 Webley revolver.

Finding that revolver, though, proved tortuous. As one lead after another dried up, the investigation ground to a standstill. For three months, the deadlock continued; then came a vital clue. An ex-convict who was being questioned in connection with a string of car thefts angrily protested his innocence, claiming that the real culprits were actually two other crooks named Browne and Kennedy. Furthermore, he'd heard them brag about killing Constable Gutteridge.

Dual Arrests

There was plenty in Browne's record to suggest that he was capable of murder; he had a long history of violence and once, while imprisoned, had brutally attacked a guard. Detectives were understandably cautious as they staked out his garage. Their patience was rewarded on January 20, 1928, when their target drove up under cover of darkness. As Browne alighted from his car, they swooped in upon him. Inside the car's glove compartment was a revolver. More guns were found indoors, together with two thousand pounds hidden in the lavatory cistern and medical instruments similar to those taken from the Morris Cowley.

Five days later in Liverpool, Kennedy was detained after a struggle in which he attempted to shoot the arresting officer (only the jamming of the gun saved the policeman's life). It was a strange reaction for someone who subsequently claimed that his role in the murder had been that of passive bystander. Browne, he said, had shot Gutteridge without any provocation. Bitterly contemptuous of his erstwhile partner's attempt to save his own neck. Browne dismissed the statement as a 'concoction'.

Within the arsenal found at Browne's garage was a .455 Webley revolver loaded with the same ancient ammunition that had killed Constable Gutteridge. When test-fired by Churchill, each cartridge revealed an identical breech block imperfection. No fewer than thirteen hundred Webley revolvers were tested in efforts to replicate the flaw, but none ever did. Churchill also noted that the black powder loaded into the Mark IV ammunition was identical to powder traces tattooed into the skin around Gutteridge's wounds.

At their trial, Browne and Kennedy were apportioned equal guilt. On May 31st 1928 Browne was hanged at Pentonville Prison, while a few miles across London, Kennedy was similarly dealt with at Wandsworth.

Reading for meaning

1   In the second paragraph of the text, what impression of Browne and Kennedy do you get? How does the writer convey this to you? *Hint: Does he seem to like them?*

2   What was the direct cause of Browne shooting PC Gutteridge? *Hint: What might Browne have thought Gutteridge was doing?*

3   What information did Robert Churchill find from the empty cartridge case discovered in the stolen car?

4   What was found at Browne's garage which suggested he was a criminal, and potentially violent?

5   Why could there be some doubt about which of the two men, Browne or Kennedy, shot PC Gutteridge? *Hint: What are the **facts** of the murder? What are the writer's **opinions**? How much relies on what Browne and Kennedy said about each other?*

Vocabulary and spelling

1   a)   In the first paragraph, what do the word 'desultory' and the phrase 'smug complacency' mean?

    b)   What do these words suggest about the writer's attitudes towards detection techniques in America and Europe at the time?

2   The writer uses a number of colourful **verbs** to catch the reader's interest and give a sense of drama and action, for example 'Browne sprang from the car'. Find three other examples of carefully-chosen verbs, and explain why they are effective.

3   The writer occasionally uses **informal** vocabulary to make the text more lively or realistic. Comment on two such usages, one in each of the paragraphs either side of the subheading 'Dual arrests'.

Sentences, paragraphs and punctuation

1   How does the structure and length of paragraph four contribute to the writer's theme? *Hint: Look at the structure, length and punctuation of the three sentences – how do they relate to the phrase 'fast moving'?*

2　In the paragraph which begins 'Finding that revolver …', how does the writer use connectives to organise and sequence that part of the narrative?

3　Why do you think the writer has split the text in two by using the subheading 'Dual Arrests'?

4　In the third paragraph from the end, the writer uses a set of brackets, a pair of commas and a set of speech marks. What does each piece of punctuation add to the meaning of the words to which it is attached?

Writing to inform, explain and describe

You have been commissioned to write a short, factual account of the Browne and Kennedy case to appear in a new encyclopaedia of crime.

Your limit is 250 words. Your audience is adults who want to know about crimes which were important because of the advances in detection they illustrate.

You will need to:

● decide what are the important **facts** of the case

● make notes about significant details about these facts

● structure your notes into an appropriate sequence

● remember the word limit.

Before handing in your final version, remember to check the following.

● Have you written an appropriate number of words on each aspect of the case, depending on their relative importance?

● Have you avoided including **opinions**? Have you stuck to the **facts**?

The Case for the Defence

Fictional detective stories were especially popular in the late nineteenth century. *The Moonstone* by Wilkie Collins (published in 1868) was the first English novel in which the plot centred on a crime and in which a detective was a main character.

Short stories about detection were also popular, especially those by Arthur Conan Doyle which recounted the exploits of Sherlock Holmes. When Doyle killed off Holmes, readers were so unhappy that he had to bring him back to life and explain away his earlier 'death' – a trick which has been copied by the writers of television soap operas, such as *Neighbours* and *Eastenders*.

Many famous novelists have tried to write murder, mystery and detective stories, including Graham Greene, the author of the next text. This is a very short story, but one which leaves you thinking for a long time – it is impossible to know exactly what has happened!

As you read

1 Think about the setting, the number of characters and the ending. Do these make this a good short story?

2 When would you guess this story is set? What are the clues which help you to come to this decision? *Hint: Look at the content (what it says) and style (how it says it).*

THE CASE FOR THE DEFENCE

It was the strangest murder trial I ever attended. They named it the Peckham murder in the headlines, though Northwood Street, where the old woman was found battered to death, was not strictly speaking in Peckham. This was not one of those cases of circumstantial evidence in which you feel the jury-men's anxiety – because mistakes *have* been made – like domes of silence muting the court. No, this murderer was all but found with the body; no one present when the Crown counsel outlined his case believed that the man in the dock stood any chance at all.

He was a heavy stout man with bulging bloodshot eyes. All his muscles seemed to be in his thighs. Yes, an ugly customer, one you wouldn't forget in a hurry – and that was an important point because the Crown proposed to call four witnesses who hadn't forgotten him, who had seen him hurrying away from the little red villa in Northwood Street. The clock had just struck two in the morning.

Mrs Salmon in 15 Northwood Street had been unable to sleep; she heard a door click shut and thought it was her own gate. So she went to the window and saw Adams (that was his name) on the steps of Mrs Parker's house. He had just come out and he was wearing gloves. He had a hammer in his hand and she saw him drop it into the laurel bushes by the front gate. But before he moved away, he had looked up – at her window. The fatal instinct that tells a man when he is watched exposed him in the light of a street-lamp to her gaze – his eyes suffused with horrifying and brutal fear, like an animal's when you raise a whip. I talked afterwards to Mrs Salmon, who naturally after the astonishing verdict went in fear herself. As I imagine did all the witnesses –

Henry MacDougall, who had been driving home from Benfleet late and nearly ran Adams down at the corner of Northwood Street. Adams was walking in the middle of the road looking dazed. And old Mr Wheeler, who lived next door to Mrs Parker, at No. 12, and was wakened by a noise – like a chair falling – through the thin-as-paper villa wall, and got up and looked out of the window, just as Mrs Salmon had done, saw Adam's back and, as he turned, those bulging eyes. In Laurel Avenue he had been seen by yet another witness – his luck was badly out; he might as well have committed the crime in broad daylight.

'I understand,' counsel said, 'that the defence proposes to plead mistaken identity. Adams's wife will tell you that he was with her at two in the morning on February 14, but after you have heard the witnesses for the Crown and examined carefully the features of the prisoner, I do not think you will be prepared to admit the possibility of mistake.'

It was all over, you would have said, but the hanging.

After the formal evidence had been given by the policeman who had found the body and the surgeon who examined it, Mrs Salmon was called. She was the ideal witness, with her slight Scotch accent and her expression of honesty, care and kindness.

The counsel for the Crown brought the story gently out. She spoke very firmly. There was no malice in her, and no sense of importance at standing there in the Central Criminal Court with a judge in scarlet hanging on her words and the reporters writing them down. Yes, she said, and then she had gone downstairs and rung up the police station.

'And do you see the man here in court?'

She looked straight at the big man in the dock, who stared hard at her with his pekingese eyes without emotion.

146

'Yes,' she said, 'there he is.'

'You are quite certain?'

She said simply, ' I couldn't be mistaken, sir.'

It was all as easy as that.

'Thank you, Mrs Salmon.'

Counsel for the defence rose to cross-examine. If you had reported as many murder trials as I have, you would have known beforehand what line he would take. And I was right, up to a point.

'Now, Mrs Salmon, you must remember that a man's life may depend on your evidence.'

'I do remember it, sir,'

'Is your eyesight good?'

'I have never had to wear spectacles, sir.'

'You are a woman of fifty-five?'

'Fifty-six, sir.'

'And the man you saw was on the other side of the road?'

'Yes, sir.'

'And it was two o'clock in the morning. You must have remarkable eyes, Mrs Salmon?'

'No, sir. There was moonlight, and when the man looked up, he had the lamplight on his face.'

'And you have no doubt whatsoever that the man you saw is the prisoner?'

I couldn't make out what he was at. He couldn't have expected any other answer than the one he got.

'None whatever, sir. It isn't a face one forgets.'

Counsel took a look round the court for a moment. Then he said, 'Do you mind, Mrs Salmon, examining again the people in court? No, not the prisoner. Stand up, please, Mr Adams,' and there at the back of the court with thick stout body and muscular legs and a pair of bulging eyes, was the exact image of the man in the dock. He was dressed the same – tight blue suit and striped tie.

'Now think very carefully, Mrs Salmon. Can you still swear that the man you saw drop the hammer in Mrs Parker's garden was the prisoner – and not this man, who is his twin brother?'

Of course she couldn't. She looked from one to the other and didn't say a word.

There the big brute sat in the dock with his legs crossed, and there he stood too at the back of the court and they both stared at Mrs Salmon. She shook her head.

What we saw then was the end of the case. There wasn't a witness prepared to swear that it was the prisoner he'd seen. And the brother? He had his alibi, too; he was with his wife.

And so the man was acquitted for lack of evidence. But whether – if he did the murder and not his brother – he was punished or not, I don't know. That extraordinary day had an extraordinary end. I followed Mrs Salmon out of court and we got wedged in the crowd who were waiting, of course, for the twins. The police tried to drive the crowd away, but all they could do was keep the road-way clear for traffic. I learned later that they tried to get the twins to leave by a back way, but they wouldn't. One of them – no one knew which – said, 'I've been acquitted, haven't I?' and they walked bang out of the front entrance. Then it happened. I don't know how, though I was only six feet away. The crowd moved and somehow one of the twins got pushed on to the road right in front of a bus.

He gave a squeal like a rabbit and that was all; he was dead, his skull smashed just as Mrs Parker's had been. Divine vengeance? I wish I knew. There was the other Adams getting on his feet from beside the body and looking straight over at Mrs Salmon. He was crying, but whether he was the murderer or the innocent man nobody will ever be able to tell. But if you were Mrs Salmon, could you sleep at night?

Reading for meaning

1 Who do you think the narrator is? Why? *Hint: What do you think the first sentence might mean? Could there be a hint in the second sentence? Is this hint supported anywhere in the third paragraph?*

2 Why does the narrator say 'It was all over, you would have said, but for the hanging'? *Hint: What does it mean? What has led him to make this judgement?*

3 How does the counsel for the defence make Mrs Salmon feel confident when she is giving her evidence? How does he trick her in the end?

4 What does the narrator feel about the Adams brothers? How does he convey this feeling to you? *Hint: Look at the words he uses to describe them, and any descriptive words which are repeated.*

5 What is the meaning of the last sentence in the text? What does it leave you thinking?

Writing to analyse, review and comment

Think of a fictional detective you know about from your reading, or from watching films or television, for example *Frost*, *Inspector Morse*, *The Bill*, *NYPD Blue*. Write about this detective in a way which would encourage other people of your age to read the books or watch the films.

In your writing, which should be about 300 words long, write three paragraphs which:

- *review* one or two of the stories which the detective has been involved in – highlight the most important and interesting aspects of them

- *comment* on how the detective works – alone or with others – and how he or she usually solves the case – by luck, through intelligent thought or through illegal methods, for example

- *analyse* why you enjoy reading about or watching this detective – is it the storylines, the characters, the settings, the writer's style?

Collect the writing from the whole class together in a booklet. You can use it to find some recommendations for reading or watching which will extend your knowledge and enjoyment of fictional detectives.

Macbeth

Although the detective story is a fairly recent literary **genre**, violent and unlawful deaths have occurred in stories since they were first told. Most of the earliest English writing which still survives is about heroic deeds in battle or against strange monsters. Greek **myths** often involve murder amongst family members or warring groups.

Shakespeare's play *Macbeth* tells such a story. Macbeth was a real person, and many of the happenings in Shakespeare's play are based on real events. However, Shakespeare altered quite a lot as well, for two reasons:

- to create a more dramatic play
- to flatter the current King, James I – some of his ancestors are characters in the play.

You are going to read the scene which opens the final act of the play. Here is a **précis** of what has happened earlier:

Macbeth is a successful general in the army of King Duncan of Scotland. On his way home from battle, he meets three witches who tell him that he will become a nobleman and then a king.

Duncan makes Macbeth Thane of Cawdor, and Lady Macbeth encourages her husband to murder the King. The Macbeths make it look as though Duncan has been murdered by his own servants. Macbeth then kills Banquo, because the witches had also predicted that Banquo's sons would become kings. He also has the wife and children of Macduff, the Thane of Fife and another possible threat to him, murdered.

Macbeth and his wife are troubled by guilt; Macbeth thinks he sees Banquo's ghost, and Lady Macbeth gradually loses her senses.

As the final act begins, one of Lady Macbeth's servants has sent for the Doctor, as she is concerned about Lady Macbeth's behaviour.

A **précis** is a shortened version of a text, which keeps all the main details but leaves out anything which does not affect these essential points.

Macbeth

Act V
Scene I   [Dunsinane. In the castle.]
Enter a Doctor of Physic and a
Waiting-Gentlewoman.

Doctor. I have two nights watched with you, but can perceive
no truth in your report. When was it she last walked?

Gentlewoman. Since his Majesty went into the field, I have seen
her rise from her bed, throw her nightgown upon her,
unlock her closet, take forth paper, fold it, write upon 't,   5
read it, afterwards seal it, and again return to bed; yet all
this while in a most fast sleep.

Doctor. A great perturbation in nature, to receive at once the
benefit of sleep and do the effects of watching! In this
slumb'ry agitation, besides her walking and other actual   10
performances, what, at any time, have your heard her say?

Gentlewoman. That, sir, which I will not report after her.

Doctor. You may to me, and 'tis most meet you should.

Gentlewoman. Neither to you nor anyone, having no witness to
confirm my speech.   15

   Enter Lady [Macbeth], with a taper.

Lo you, here she comes! This is her very guise, and, upon
my life, fast asleep! Observe her; stand close.

Doctor. How came she by that light?

Gentlewoman. Why, it stood by her. She has light by her
continually. 'Tis her command.   20

Doctor. You see, her eyes are open.

Gentlewoman. Ay, but their sense are shut.

Doctor. What is it she does now? Look, how she rubs her hands.

Gentlewoman. It is an accustomed action with her, to seem   25
thus washing her hands: I have known her continue in this a quarter of an hour.

Lady Macbeth. Yet here's a spot.

Doctor. Hark! She speaks. I will set down what comes from her, to satisfy my remembrance the more strongly.   30

Lady Macbeth. Out, damned spot! Out I say! One: two: why, then 'tis time to do 't. Hell is murky. Fie, my lord, fie! A soldier, and afeard? What need we fear who knows it, when none can call our pow'r to accompt? Yet who would have thought the old man to have had so much blood in him?   35

Doctor. Do you mark that?

Lady Macbeth. The Thane of Fife had a wife. Where is she now? What, will these hands ne'er be clean? No more o' that, my lord, no more o' that! You mar all with this starting.

Doctor. Go to, go to! You have known what you should not.   40

Gentlewoman. She has spoke what she should not, I am sure of that. Heaven knows what she has known.

Lady Macbeth. Here's the smell of the blood still. All the perfumes of Arabia will not sweeten this little hand. Oh, oh, oh!   45

Doctor. What a sigh is there! The heart is sorely charged.

Gentlewoman. I would not have such a heart in my bosom for the dignity of the whole body.

Doctor. Well, well, well—

Gentlewoman. Pray God it be, sir.   50

Doctor. This disease is beyond my practice. Yet I have known those which have walked in their sleep who have died holily in their beds.

Lady Macbeth. Wash your hands; put on your nightgown;
look not so pale! I tell you yet again, Banquo's buried.   55
He cannot come out on 's grave.

Doctor. Even so?

Lady Macbeth. To bed, to bed! There's knocking at the gate.
Come, come, come, come, give me your hand! What's done
cannot be undone. To bed, to bed, to bed!   60

        Exit Lady [Macbeth]

Doctor. Will she go now to bed?

Gentlewoman. Directly.

Doctor. Foul whisp'rings are abroad. Unnatural deeds
Do breed unnatural troubles. Infected minds
To their deaf pillows will discharge their secrets.   65
More needs she the divine than the physician.
God, God forgive us all! Look after her;
Remove from her the means of all annoyance,
And still keep eyes upon her. So good night.

Reading for meaning

1 According to the Gentlewoman, what sort of things has Lady Macbeth been doing while sleepwalking?

2 What is the Gentlewoman's attitude towards the Doctor? Why do you think she behaves like this towards him?

3 What is Lady Macbeth talking about in this scene? Why does she mention these things in this way? *Hint: Remember the* **précis** *of the events leading up to this scene.*

4 How does the Gentlewoman feel towards Lady Macbeth?

5 What does the Doctor fear might happen to Lady Macbeth?

Shakespeare's dramatic techniques

1 What is the atmosphere during this scene? How does Shakespeare build it up before Lady Macbeth enters? *Hint: Think about the setting, what is being talked about, who is on stage.*

2 Lady Macbeth does not speak for some time after her entrance. Why do you think this is? What effect does it have?

3 In lines 16–27, why do you think the Doctor and the Gentlewoman describe what Lady Macbeth is doing, when the audience could see it for themselves? *Hint: Think about stage performances compared with television close-ups – why are details of what she does here so important?*

4 How does Shakespeare make you realise that Lady Macbeth's mind is disturbed? *Hint: Look at what she does, what she says, how she says it.*

5 How does Shakespeare leave the audience in a state of suspense at the end of the scene?

Shakespeare's language

1 Many words and expressions used in Shakespeare's time are either not used at all today, or have changed in meaning. Draw up a table like the one opposite and use it to list any such words in this extract.

(You may have already started this table when you looked at the extract from *A Midsummer Night's Dream* on page 120.)

You can add to this table as you read other extracts from Shakespeare's plays.

Title of play	Language no longer used		Changed language		
	Word	Meaning	Word	Shakespearian meaning	Modern meaning

2 Work on the section of the text allocated to you by your teacher. Rewrite it in modern English. Try to keep the meaning and atmosphere as close to the original as possible.

Drama

1 In your group, prepare this scene from Macbeth so you are ready to act it out for the rest of the class.

You will need:

● someone to be the director

● three people to play the different roles.

Think about the role of the director and how he or she can help the actors.

2 Prepare the scene again, this time in modern English. You will need to prepare the text first – look back at activity 2 in 'Shakespeare's language' above.

Choose someone else in the group to be the director this time.

3 When you have seen all the performances, vote on which was the best.

● Did more people prefer the original version? Or was the modern version more popular?

● Why did the class like one version better than another?

Writing to explore, imagine and entertain

You are *either* the Doctor or the Gentlewoman. It is later the same day. Write a letter to a trusted friend, describing what you have seen and asking for advice about what to do. You may wish to write in Shakespearian language, but you may use modern English if you prefer.

A text from a different culture

I like to stay up

In the last text in this chapter, we return to the idea of being scared by books we read. Do creepy stories sometimes frighten you? Read the poem opposite by Grace Nichols, who was born in Guyana in the Caribbean.

Reading for meaning

When you have read the poem, answer these questions.

1 Why does the speaker like to stay up?

2 Which three words convey the feelings that the jumbie stories give the speaker? Which do you think is the best word?

3 Why does the speaker call the jumbie stories 'stupid' towards the end of the poem?

4 How does the structure of the last five stanzas help you believe that the speaker is really scared? *Hint: Think about repetition and* **rhyme**.

5 How much do you know about the speaker after you have read this poem?

I like to stay up

I like to stay up
and list
when big people talking
jumbie* stories

I does feel   5
So tingly and excited
inside me

But when my mother say
'Girl, time for bed'

Then is when   10
I does feel a dread

Then is when
I does jump into bed

Then is when
I does cover up   15
from me feet to me head

Then is when
I does wish I didn't listen
to no stupid jumbie story

Then is when   20
I does wish I did read
me book instead

*'Jumbie' is a Guyanese word for 'ghost'

Language variation

The poem is not written in **standard English**, but in a **dialect**. Find places where the dialect differs from standard English. Look for:

- a word which we would not use at all in standard English

- a possessive pronoun used once in its standard form and four times in a non-standard form

- non-standard verb forms.

Make sure you understand this. You need to know the differences between any non-standard forms used in this poem and what the standard forms would be, so you can do the next piece of work on your own.

Writing to inform, explain and describe

1 Rewrite the poem 'I like to stay up' **as** a paragraph in standard English prose.

Remember the discussion about the poem, and think carefully about:

- what non-standard language forms you will need to change

- how you will need to change the structure of the original text, for example, by adding punctuation and taking out repetition.

2 In a second paragraph, say which is the more enjoyable text to read – the original poem or your prose version. Why do you think this is so?

You should write about:

- which version creates a better sense of fear, and why

- how important the structure and **rhythm** of the poem is, or whether the prose version is easier to understand.

Review

What did you particularly enjoy in this chapter?

What did you not like very much?

Was there anything:
- you found difficult to understand?
- you discovered or understood for the first time?

Use this checklist to help you answer these questions and to review the progress you have made.

- **You have read**: two modern poems; a story written in the style of a traditional tale; an extract from a nineteenth-century novel and a modern short story; extracts from two plays by Shakespeare; part of a non-fiction information text.

- **You have thought about how writers use**: old and modern forms of language; internal rhyme and repetition; different viewpoints to tell a story and dramatic techniques in a playscript; text types or genres such as fairy stories, legends, traditional tales, ballads, and crime stories.

- **You have written to**: imagine, explore and entertain – a ballad, a letter and part of a narrative; inform, explain and describe – an encyclopaedia entry, an article about language change and an account of a poem; persuade, argue and advise – a statement by a fictional character; analyse, review and comment – a review of a detective story or film.

- **To improve your writing, you have thought about**: word families and spellings; verb tenses; how punctuation can be used to affect meaning and response; précis.

- **Your speaking and listening work has included**: dramatising and performing a text as a radio play; rehearsing and performing a scene from Shakespeare; group reading of a poem; selecting, preparing and relating an anecdote; evaluating your own and others' work.

- **You may have used ICT to**: make an alphabetical word list; research into, and make a chart of, Shakespearian language; create a ballad broadsheet; spellcheck, and present final drafts of your writing neatly and attractively.

4 Winners and losers

The texts in this chapter describe the highs and lows of life. They are set in different times and cultures – some are very serious, others may make you smile or even laugh aloud.

Before you start to read

Discuss the following questions with a partner. Agree on some ideas that you can contribute to a class discussion.

1 What does it mean when you call someone a winner or a loser?

2 What can make a person a winner or a loser? For example, is it their family life, their work, their wealth or their view of life?

3 Is it important to be a winner rather than a loser? Why? Think about how you would feel if someone called you a loser.

4 Think of some examples of winners and losers you have come across in books, films or television series. How are they presented? What do you feel about them?

5 Think of some well-known examples of winners and losers in real life. How do you get to know about them? How are your views of them guided, for example, by how they are represented in the media?

4.1 Poetry and drama

King Henry V

One obvious situation where there could be winners and losers is in a fight – or, on a national scale, in a battle or a war.

The first text in this chapter comes from Shakespeare's *King Henry V*, set against the background of the Hundred Years War between England and France in the fourteenth and fifteenth centuries.

Both this text and the one that follows were written long after the wars they describe, but they are equally successful in giving you an idea of the demands war makes on military leaders – how the leaders know the importance of winning and losing, for themselves and for future generations, and the cost of winning or losing.

In Shakespeare's King Henry V, *the young King is determined to lead his troops in the attack on the French town of Harfleur. As the scaling-ladders are set against the town walls, Henry addresses his troops in one of the most famous inspirational speeches ever written.*

Reading for meaning

When you have read the text, answer these questions.

1 What does Henry say that people should be like in peace time?

2 What image does he use, starting in line 6, to describe how soldiers should behave in war? Is it a good image? *Hint: Look back to page 59 to remind yourself about* **imagery**.

3 What does Henry say about the soldiers' ancestors? *Hint: Look at the whole of the passage from line 17 to line 30.*

4 In line 28, Henry uses a particular trick of **rhetoric** to encourage the soldiers. What does he do? Why might this be an effective way of firing them up for the battle?

KING HENRY V

ACT III.

SCENE I. – *France. Before Harfleur.*

Alarum. Enter KING HENRY, EXETER, BEDFORD, GLOUCESTER, *and Soldiers with scaling-ladders*

K. Hen. Once more unto the breach, dear friends, once more,
    Or close the wall up with our English dead.
    In peace there's nothing so becomes a man
    As modest stillness and humility:
    But when the blast of war blows in our ears,   5
    Then imitate the action of the tiger;
    Stiffen the sinews, conjure up the blood,
    Disguise fair nature with hard-favour'd rage;
    Then lend the eye a terrible aspect;
    Let it pry through the portage of the head   10
    Like the brass cannon; let the brow o'erwhelm it
    As fearfully as doth a galled rock
    O'erhang and jutty his confounded base,
    Swill'd with the wild and wasteful ocean.
    Now set the teeth and stretch the nostril wide,   15
    Hold hard the breath, and bend up every spirit
    To his full height! On, on, you noblest English!
    Whose blood is fet from fathers of war-proof;
    Fathers that, like so many Alexanders,
    Have in these parts from morn till even fought,   20
    And sheath'd their swords for lack of argument.
    Dishonour not your mothers; now attest
    That those whom you call'd fathers did beget you.
    Be copy now to men of grosser blood,
    And teach them how to war. And you, good yeomen,   25
    Whose limbs were made in England, show us here
    The mettle of your pasture; let us swear
    That you are worth your breeding; which I doubt not;
    For there is none of you so mean and base
    That hath not noble lustre in your eyes.   30
    I see you stand like greyhounds in the slips,
    Straining upon the start. The game's afoot:
    Follow your spirit; and upon this charge
    Cry, "God for Harry, England, and Saint George!"

        [Exeunt. Alarum, and chambers go off.

Rhetoric is the art of speaking or writing with the aim of persuading the audience, often by using:

- exaggerated language (such as **imagery**)
- devices such as **rhetorical questions** or suggestions (such as Henry makes in this speech) which raise a possible problem (in this case, the soldiers' lack of desire for the fight) in order to squash it.

Shakespeare's speeches

1   What features in this speech might have helped to make it famous? *Hint: Think about the situation, what Henry says and how he says it.*

2   If you were one of the soldiers, would this speech inspire you? Why?

3   What does the speech tell you about people's attitudes to war and fighting for your country in Shakespeare's time? *Hint: Is there any suggestion that Henry and the English troops might be doing the wrong thing?*

4   How does Henry end his speech effectively? *Hint: Look at the contrast – emphasised by the punctuation – between the length of phrases in the last two and a half lines and in the earlier part of the speech. What could you say about the final words of the last two lines? Why is the last sentence put inside speech marks? What does the exclamation mark do?*

5   What typical features of Shakespearian **blank verse** can you find in this speech? What effects are achieved by variations in the regular pattern?

Blank verse is when poetry has a regular rhythm or metre, but has no rhyme. Shakespeare often writes in blank verse, and generally uses a rhythmic structure known as the **iambic pentameter**:
- 'Iambic' describes a unit of two beats – an unstressed (or 'weak') syllable followed by a stressed (or 'strong') syllable, i.e. dee-**dum**.
- 'Pentameter' means that there are five of these units in each line.
The writer may vary the number of beats per line, and the sequence of stressed and unstressed beats, to give a particular emphasis or effect.

Shakespeare's language

Many words and phrases used in Shakespeare's time are either not used at all today, or have changed in meaning. Draw up a table like the one below and use it to list any such words in this extract.

(You may already have started this table when you looked at the extracts from *A Midsummer Night's Dream*, page 120, and *Macbeth*, pages 154–5.)

Title of play	Language no longer used		Changed language		
	Word	Meaning	Word	Shakespearian meaning	Modern meaning

You can add to this table as you read other extracts from Shakespeare's plays.

Writing to inform, explain and describe

Imagine that you are a reporter for a newspaper during the Hundred Years War. Write an report of King Henry's speech and describe the effect it had on the troops.

Writing to persuade, argue and advise

Write a letter to the same newspaper from someone who has read your report, but who feels the war is pointless and that the English army should leave France. If you wish, you could be someone who has lost close relatives in the war or whose ancestors came from France. Make the letter as persuasive as you can.

The Devil's Disciple

Although George Bernard Shaw's play *The Devil's Disciple* is set during the American War of Independence in the eighteenth century, no battle scenes are staged. The progress of the war is simply reported from time to time. The real subject of the play is how honest people are about themselves, their motives and their actions.

The hero of the play, Dick Dudgeon, is considered by many to be an immoral and untrustworthy young man. However, when some British soldiers arrive to arrest the local minister, Antony Anderson, because they suspect him of being a member of the rebel army, Dick pretends to be Anderson and is prepared to go through with the deception and to be hanged in his place.

As his trial draws near, the two senior officers who will conduct the hearing against Dick, General Burgoyne and Major Swindon, talk about their task and the war in general. The two men have never met before.

THE DEVIL'S DISCIPLE

BURGOYNE. Major Swindon, I presume.

SWINDON. Yes. General Burgoyne, if I mistake not. [*They bow to one another ceremoniously*]. I am glad to have the support of your presence this morning. It is not particularly lively business hanging this poor devil of a minister.

BURGOYNE. [*throwing himself into Swindon's chair*] No, sir, it's not. It is making too much of the fellow to execute him: what more could you have done if he had been a member of the Church of England? Martyrdom, sir, is what these people like: it is the only way in which a man can become famous without ability. However, you have committed us to hanging him; and the sooner he is hanged the better.

SWINDON We have arranged it for 12 o'clock. Nothing remains to be done except to try him.

BURGOYNE. [*looking at him with suppressed anger*] Nothing – except to save your own necks, perhaps. Have you heard the news from Springtown?

SWINDON. Nothing special. The latest reports are satisfactory.

BURGOYNE.[*rising in amazement*] Satisfactory, sir! Satisfactory!! [*He stares at him for a moment, and then adds, with grim intensity*] I am glad you take that view of them.

SWINDON. [*puzzled*] Do I understand that in your opinion –

BURGOYNE. I do not express my opinion. I never stoop to that habit of profane language which unfortunately coarsens our profession. If I did, sir, perhaps I should be able to express my opinion of the news from Springtown – the news which y o u [*severely*] have apparently not heard. How soon do you get news from your supports here? – in the course of a month, eh?

SWINDON. [*turning sulky*] I suppose the reports have been taken to you, sir, instead of to me. Is there anything serious?

BURGOYNE.[*taking a report from his pocket and holding it up*] Springtown's in the hands of the rebels. [*He throws the report on the table*].

SWINDON. [*aghast*] Since yesterday!

BURGOYNE. Since two o'clock this morning. Perhaps we shall be in their hands before two o'clock tomorrow morning. Have you thought of that?

SWINDON. [*confidently*] As to that, General, the British soldier will give a good account of himself.

BURGOYNE.[*bitterly*] And therefore, I suppose, sir, the British officer need not know his business: the British soldier will get him out of all his blunders with the bayonet. In future, sir, I must ask you to be a little less generous with the blood of your men, and a little more generous with your own brains.

SWINDON. I am sorry I cannot pretend to your intellectual eminence, sir. I can only do my best, and rely on the devotion of my countrymen.

BURGOYNE.[*suddenly becoming suavely sarcastic*] May I ask are you writing a melodrama, Major Swindon?

SWINDON. [*flushing*] No, sir.

BURGOYNE. What a pity! W h a t a pity! [*Dropping his sarcastic tone and facing him suddenly and seriously*] Do you at all realize, sir, that we have nothing standing between us and destruction but our own bluff and the sheepishness of these colonists? They are men of the same English stock as ourselves: six to one of us [*repeating it emphatically*] six to one, sir; and nearly half our troops are Hessians, Brunswickers, German dragoons, and Indians with scalping knives. These are the countrymen on whose devotion you rely! Suppose the colonists find a leader! Suppose the news from Springtown should turn out to mean that they have already found a leader! What shall we do then? Eh?

SWINDON. [*sullenly*] Our duty, sir, I presume.

BURGOYNE. [*again sarcastic – giving him up as a fool*] Quite so, quite so. Thank you, Major Swindon, thank you. Now youve settled the question, sir – thrown a flood of light on the situation. What a comfort to me to feel that I have at my side so devoted and able an officer to support me in this emergency! I think, sir, it will probably relieve both our feelings if we proceed to hang this dissenter without further delay [*he strikes the bell*] especially as I am debarred by my principles from the customary military vent for my feelings. [*The sergeant appears*]. Bring your man in.

SARGEANT. Yes, sir.

BURGOYNE.And mention to any officer you may meet that the court cannot wait any longer for him.

SWINDON. [*keeping his temper with difficulty*] The staff is perfectly ready, sir. They have been waiting your convenience for fully half an hour. P e r f e c t l y ready, sir.

BURGOYNE. [*blandly*] So am I.

Reading for meaning

1 How do the first few speeches made by each man establish his character? What are the obvious differences between them?

2 Swindon annoys Burgoyne. Why? *Hint: Look at what he says and how he says it.*

3 What in this scene make it clear to you that Burgoyne is more intelligent than Swindon?

4 What does Burgoyne feel about the skills and loyalty of the British army? How does he constrast this with the qualities of the American rebels? *Hint: What does his long speech about the soldiers tell us about his personal attitude towards the war? Does this conflict with his professional attitude?*

5 What do the last three speeches in this scene tell you about Burgoyne?

Melodrama

Shaw called *The Devil's Disciple* a **melodrama**. At one point in the extract General Burgoyne makes a sarcastic reference to the **genre**. Why do you think he makes this comment to Major Swindon at that moment? What does he mean by it?

> **Melodrama** describes a type of play, especially popular in the nineteenth century, which has a simple plot of good triumphing over evil, and often a poor or humble hero getting the better of a rich or upper-class villain. *The Devil's Disciple* contains features of melodrama in the character transformation of Dick Dudgeon and in his dramatic reprieve from hanging at the very end.

Vocabulary and spelling

George Bernard Shaw was one of many people who, through the ages, have suggested changing the spelling of many English words to make them more straightforward. He favoured (or favored!) 'American' spellings of words, such as 'color' and 'honor', and he disliked using apostrophes in words such as 'shant' and 'dont' – although he still used apostrophes in 'I'm' and 'it's'!

He was also very particular about the layout and printing of his plays. For example, he insisted that stage directions were always printed in italics and put inside square brackets. This led to a problem: italics were traditionally used to show that a word should be emphasised. To avoid confusion with stage directions, Shaw asked printers to space out the letters of words which he wanted actors to stress.

1 Look in the text for examples of where Shaw has:
   a) omitted an apostrophe
   b) used spacing to indicate that a word is important.

2 There are no examples in this text of altered spellings. However, there are a number of words which you may feel could be made more simple by adjusting the spelling. Make a list of any such words and suggest alternative, simplified spellings for them. What problems might the simplified spelling lead to?

Spelling rules in English may seem both difficult and inconsistent – but it is worth learning them!
- If you are aware of families of words, origins of words (sometimes from other languages) and similarities between words, you will soon become a more accurate speller.
- You can also learn words by:
  - sounding the letter combinations carefully when you see them written down
  - memorising words which you know cause you difficulties
  - keeping a personal spelling log. Your log should contain lists of words that you find difficult, notes of common spelling rules, investigations into spelling, and learning techniques such as look-cover-write.

Remember that dictionaries are useful for checking, as are spellcheck devices on computers – but they will not always suggest the correct word!

Writing to persuade, argue and advise

Using material from your work on the 'Vocabulary and spelling' activity opposite, write an article for a teenage magazine in which you propose, illustrate and justify a number of changes to the English system of spelling to make it easier for learners and users of the language.

Writing to analyse, review and comment

1   Read someone else's proposal for changes to the English spelling system.

2   Write a reply for the same magazine, either agreeing with the ideas or criticising them. Give detailed reasons in either case.

Drama

The text you have read is an extract from a play, but it consists of just two people talking to each other, and a brief entrance by a third character at the end. How could a director in the theatre make the scene dramatic and hold the audience's attention?

1   Prepare a section of this scene for performance (about 20–30 lines) so that it comes across in an interesting and dramatic way.

   Think about:

   ● the way you want the characters to come across, and how to make them different

   ● how to use movement

   ● the importance of facial expressions and gestures

   ● the need for any props

   ● how **tone**, pace and volume may affect the meaning.

2   Watch the other groups perform their section of the scene. Think about how successful each is at conveying a real sense of character and conflict to the audience.

3   When you have watched all the groups, discuss these questions with the rest of the class:

   ● Is any one interpretation of the characters best?

   ● Is it possible to act out the scene in different ways?

Ozymandias

The next text is a well-known poem by Percy Bysshe Shelley, a famous English **Romantic poet**.

'Ozymandias' is about a ruler of an ancient civilisation. It is set in a barren but spectacular setting, and it puts across its main idea through telling, in outline, the story of its subject's life and death.

Ozymandias of Egypt

I met a traveller from an antique land
Who said: Two vast and trunkless legs of stone
Stand in the desert. Near them on the sand,
Half sunk, a shatter'd visage lies, whose frown
And wrinkled lip and sneer of cold command   5
Tell that its sculptor well those passions read
Which yet survive, stamp'd on these lifeless things,
The hand that mock'd them and the heart that fed;
And on the pedestal these words appear:
'My name is Ozymandias, king of kings: 10
Look on my works, ye Mighty, and despair!'
Nothing beside remains. Round the decay
Of that colossal wreck, boundless and bare,
The lone and level sands stretch far away.

The **Romantic poets** were a group which included John Keats, Samuel Taylor Coleridge and William Wordsworth. They lived and worked in the first part of the nineteenth century. They were particularly interested in the English countryside and in telling dramatic stories in verse – you may have come across Coleridge's 'Rime of the Ancient Mariner'. These poets also shared an interest in the ancient civilisations of Greece, Rome and, as in this poem, Egypt.

Reading for meaning

1 What has the traveller seen in the desert? *Hint: Facts, not opinions!*

2 What example does the traveller to show that he thinks the sculptor was particularly skilled?

3 What does line 8 mean? *Hint: Whose hand and heart? What does 'them' refer to?*

4 What sort of king do you think Ozymandias was? What is the evidence for your views?

5 What do the last three lines describe? How does this contrast with the earlier description of the king? *Hint: Think about **irony**.*

6 Why do you think Shelley chose this subject to write about?

7 What typical features of a **sonnet** can you identify in this poem?

8 a) Find two examples of **alliteration** and two examples of **onomatopoeia** in this poem.
   b) Are they effective? If so, explain why in each case.

A **sonnet** is a poem of 14 lines with a specific rhyming scheme. Sonnets are often, but not always, about human emotions such as love. The first part is often a description of a place, an object or a feeling leading up to the main idea or 'message' which is expressed towards the end.

Research activity

Carry out some research on Shelley. Produce an A3 information sheet, including appropriate illustrations.

Vocabulary and spelling

1 Look at the ways in which Shelley uses apostrophes. Why do you think he does this?

2 What is the meaning of these three words as they are used in the poem: 'antique', 'visage', 'colossal'. *Hint: Are they still used nowadays? Has their meaning changed at all? Where do the words come from? Can you see any links with other languages?*

Poetic diction describes the range of language used in poems. It may include:

- **archaic** (old-fashioned) words, such as 'damsel' instead of 'girl' or ''twas' instead of 'it was'
- words which are now usually only used in poetry, such as 'slumber' for 'sleep'
- words invented by writers, known as neologisms, for example 'lovescape', invented by Gerard Manley Hopkins on the model of 'landscape'
- original and striking word combinations, such as 'a grief ago' used by Dylan Thomas to suggest how someone has been continually grieving.

Writing to inform, explain and describe

Think about the **ironic** main idea in 'Ozymandias': that in the end, no matter how powerful the ruler may have been in his lifetime, all that remains of him now is a broken statue in the desert.

Write a paragraph (about 10 or 12 lines) in which you express an ironic viewpoint about a setting or a person. For example, it could be:

- a fairground which has been colourful and cheerful the night before, but now is the scene of a murder enquiry, or

- a sportsperson who has won countless honours but is now the victim of a wasting illness, or

- a public figure despised by most people who, in private, is a loving family person.

This piece of writing is a real challenge: keep it brief, and keep to the point. Make the contrast which provides the irony clear, and don't confuse it with unnecessary detail. Think how much Shelley says in just over 100 words!

A Poison Tree

This is a poem by William Blake, who lived around the turn of the eighteenth and nineteenth centuries. He was an early member of the same group of poets as Shelley, the **Romantics**. As well as being a poet, Blake was a fine artist, and much of his work – both poetry and pictures – is about biblical, religious or moral themes.

A Poison Tree

I was angry with my friend:
I told my wrath, my wrath did end.
I was angry with my foe:
I told it not, my wrath did grow.

And I watered it in fears,   5
Night and morning with my tears;
And I sunned it with smiles,
And with soft deceitful wiles.

And it grew both day and night,
Till it bore an apple bright;   10
And my foe beheld it shine,
And he knew that it was mine,

And into my garden stole
When the night had veiled the pole:
In the morning glad I see   15
My foe outstretched beneath the tree.

Reading for meaning

1 What is the basic idea of the poem, expressed in stanza 1? Why do you think the rest of the poem develops lines 3 and 4 rather than lines 1 and 2? *Hint: Does this emphasise in any way what stanza 1 actually says?*

2 a) What two different types of behaviour shown by an angry person are described in stanza 2?
   b) What does this suggest about the way people may behave when they are 'bottling up' anger?

3 What does the 'apple' in stanza 3 represent or **symbolise**?

4 a) What two meanings might the word 'stole' have in stanza 5?
   b) How do these two possible meanings add to the richness of the text?

5 Why do you think Blake chose the title 'A Poison Tree' for this poem? *Hint: Think about **metaphor**.*

Blake's poetic technique

1 Describe the **rhythm** and **rhyme** schemes used in this poem. Is this simple structure effective or not? *Hint: Think of types of poems you may know which follow similar simple patterns. How is this simplicity helpful to the reader or listener?*

2 What do you need to do when you are reading line 7 to make it fit the metre? *Hint: Think back to the question about the use of the apostrophe in Shelley's poem.*

3 Look at all the repetitive structures in the first stanza – these involve single words, phrases, whole lines and couplets.
   a) How is repetition used in the rest of the poem?
   b) Is there a point at which you expect repetition, but it doesn't come? What is the effect of this? Hint: Think about the last stanza, and its importance to the meaning of the poem.

4 The poem is written in the past tense, but in line 15 changes to the present tense. What is the effect of this change?

5 In line 10, the words 'apple bright' have been **inverted** (written in the opposite order from how we would normally use them). Why do you think Blake did this? *Hint: Think about the meaning and the structure of the poem.*

> **Word order** is important in most languages, and sometimes has to follow very strict rules. For example, in French, adjectives usually follow the noun they describe, while in English the adjective normally comes before the noun.
>
> • Sometimes, word order can be varied to give particular emphasis or to achieve another effect, such as surprise.
>
> • **Inversion**, that is, reversing the usual order of words, may be used in poetry to help the writer to make a rhyme, or to put particular emphasis on an important word by placing it in a more prominent position. In line 10 of 'A Poison Tree', Blake achieves both of these purposes at once by writing 'apple bright' instead of 'bright apple'.

Speaking and listening

1 In your group, devise a choral reading of 'A Poison Tree'. Although it appears to be a very simple text, think about the different effects you could achieve by:

● the dramatic contrast of single and multiple voices

● varying the tone

● varying the pace and volume.

2 When you have heard the other groups read, discuss as a class the various interpretations of the text. Are some more successful than others? Why?

Texts from different cultures

The Village by the Sea

The first text in this section is an extract from *The Village by the Sea*, a novel by Anita Desai. It tells the story of Hari and his sister, Lila, who are the eldest children of a poor Indian family in the village of Thul.

The children's mother is very ill, and their father is a drunkard. A large industrial company wants to build a fertiliser factory near the village, which will ruin the farming and fishing trade on which the villagers and people from the nearby town of Alibagh depend.

Hari joins a protest march to Bombay with some of the villagers. He is totally unprepared for what the city is like, the noise, the dirt and the crowds, the rudeness of the police and the process of political protest.

The Village by the Sea

He was silenced by awe when he saw the city of Bombay looming over their boats and the oily green waves. He would have liked to stand and stare as he disembarked from the boat at the Sassoon docks, aching and stiff from the long ride in the jam-packed boat, but there was no time, no leisure for that. His fellow passengers were pushing and shoving and jostling past him and he was carried along by them. They pushed and shoved because they were in turn being pushed and shoved by the Bombay crowds that thronged the docks – people in a hurry to get something done, so many people in such a great hurry as the villagers had never seen before. It was only out of the corner of his eye that he saw, briefly, before being pushed on, the great looming sides of steamships berthed at the docks, cranes lifting and lowering huge bales, men bare-bodied and sweating carrying huge packing cases, boxes and baskets on their heads and shoulders, grunting as they hurried, women like the fisherwomen at home with their purple and green saris tucked up between their legs as they ran with baskets of shining, slithering fish from the boats to the market, straw and mud and fish scales making the ground dangerously slippery. Added to this chaos were the smells of the city mingling with the familiar smells of the sea and fish and turning them into something strange, and the noises of the city – not only the familiar fishermen's voices, loud and ringing, but the noise of the traffic which was so rarely heard in or around Thul.

And now they were out through the gates and on the street and in the midst of the terrifying traffic. In all his life Hari had not seen so much traffic as he saw in that one moment on that one street. In Thul there was only an occasional bus driving down the main road of the village to the

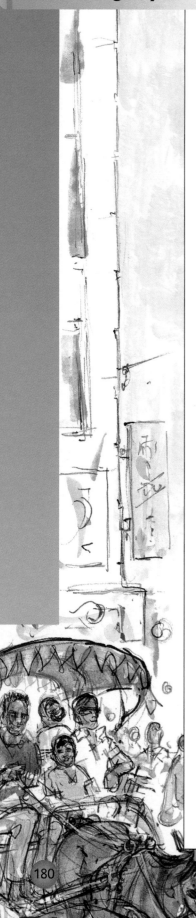

highway, and very rarely a single, dusty car. When he went to Alibagh, it was chiefly bicycles that he saw, and a few cycle-rickshaws, and of course buses and lorries. But here there was everything at once as if all the traffic in the world had met on the streets of Bombay – cycles, rickshaws, hand-carts, tongas, buses, cars, taxis and lorries – hooting and screeching and grinding and roaring past and around him. He clutched the arm of the man next to him in alarm and then was relieved to find it was a farmer from Thul, Mahe.

"Hurry, brother – don't stop – come, we have to go to the *Kala Ghoda*, the Black Horse," Mahe panted, and together they dodged the traffic and ran straight into a huge red double-decker bus that screeched to a halt just before their noses. The driver leant out of the window and bellowed at them. They stood transfixed, shaking.

Then the police appeared – the famed Bombay police who, with a wave of their batons and a blast on their whistles, could bring the traffic to a halt or send it up one road and down another, and were capable even of controlling processions and herding marchers through the crowded city such as this one of fishermen from Alibagh.

"Where have you come from, fool?" the policeman roared at Hari. "Never seen traffic lights? Don't you know how to cross a street? Come straight from the pumpkin fields, have you?"

"Send him back there – let him grow pumpkins – keep him off the Bombay streets," shouted the bus driver fiercely.

The policeman laughed, held up his hand to keep the bus waiting and waved to the marchers to cross the road.

"We are farmers and fishermen from Alibagh," said Mahe quietly before he moved on. "We have come to speak to the Chief Minister."

"You do that," the policeman told him. "You do that – he is waiting for you, with tea and a garland and a sweet for each of you." He burst out laughing again, winking at the bus-driver as he did so, and then blew his whistle shrilly to make them move. Hari and his companion moved on, very hurt and offended.

"These Bombay-*wallahs*, the rudest people on earth," muttered Mahe, and Hari nodded.

Those were only the first jeers of the day. They were to hear many more as they walked through the streets to the mysterious Black Horse. As Hari looked up fearfully at the towering buildings, ten and twenty storeys high, at the huge shops and their windows that were as large as the huts at home and much brighter, and pushed past the people who teemed on the streets more plentifully than fish in the sea, he wondered about the Black Horse. Did this amazing city contain a great black horse as a kind of deity, a god? He looked for it eagerly, perhaps a little anxiously, but saw only people, buildings and traffic, and heard only the honking of horns, the grinding of gears and the roar of the great double-decker buses, the taxis and cars. People pushed past with their market bags, hand bags and brief cases, grumbling, "Here's another procession to hold us up," and, "What is this lot shouting for now? We'll miss the bus – we'll be late for work – here, get out of my way."

Once another procession passed directly in front of theirs and they had to stop and wait till it wound past them. To Hari's utter amazement, all the people marching in it were women. They held up banners, raised their fists in the air and shouted, "Bring down the prices! We want oil! We want sugar! We want rice at fair prices!" and "Long live Women's Society for Freedom and Justice!" Then all the women would shout in one voice, "*Jai!*" and surge forwards. At their head was a grey-haired old lady who waved not her fist but a wooden rolling-pin in the air and all the others laughed and cheerfully encouraged her to hold it high and wave it. Some held cooking pots and beat on them with long-handled cooking spoons, making a great din that they seemed to be thoroughly enjoying.

Hari and the other Alibagh villagers stood open-mouthed in amazement: they had not brought along a single woman with them, had not thought it necessary, had been sure that they the

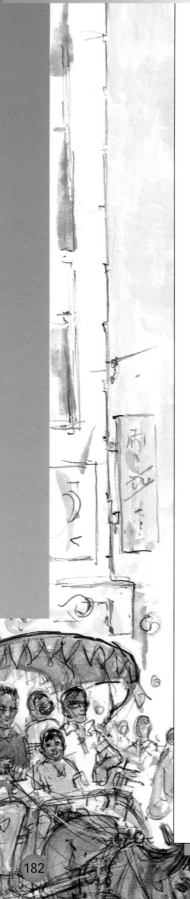

menfolk, could manage it all on their own and the women would only be a nuisance. Here in Bombay it seemed women did not trust men to manage for them, and they were determined to organise their affairs themselves. It was a very strange new idea to Hari and he did not join in the laughter or the jokes that followed in their wake, but walked on soberly after they had passed, wondering what his mother and Lila would have thought of it.

Now they had the policemen flanking them, waving their batons and keeping them in orderly rows. It seemed they were quite used to such processions and knew exactly how to handle them and direct them. Hari found they were being led around a large circle around which were great domed buildings surrounded by parks and trees. "Look, look, the museum," someone cried, and another asked excitedly, "Will we be able to visit it?" But no, they were being led to a square between large, old, grey office buildings and there, in the centre of the square, was an empty pedestal. "Black Horse. Black Horse," Hari heard the men saying and he asked, "But where is it?". "Don't you know?" someone said. "It was taken away when the British left – the people of Bombay did not want to see a foreign ruler after independence, not even a stone one." "Oh," said Hari in gravest disappointment, for he would dearly have liked to see the emperor upon his horse. He stood stock-still, staring at the empty pedestal and trying to picture the black horse on it, while the other villagers came to stand beside him. The traffic continued to pour around them as if no one cared why they had come or what they were doing here.

A wooden ladder had been set up beside the pedestal and a thin, elderly man with a white beard, a stranger to the men from Alibagh, climbed onto it. He held a megaphone to his mouth and began to speak. Hari tried to ignore the traffic, the horns blaring and the wheels churning, and to catch a few words of the speech.

"I have come here to speak to you, and speak for you, because I believe in your way of life, because your green fields and the sea are valuable to all of us as they are to you. Our trees, our fish, our cattle and birds have to be protected …"

Hari wondered who he was and why he spoke so passionately. He looked like a city man – neat, clean and educated – not like a man from the village used to rough work in the sun and dust. Yet he spoke of fish and cattle and trees with feeling and concern. Why did he care so much?

As if he had heard Hari's thoughts, he answered, "You may wonder why I, a citizen of Bombay, care to join my brothers from the village and speak in their cause. Maybe you do not trust me to speak for you. In a way, you are right because I do have selfish reasons. All the citizens of Bombay are concerned. These factories that are to come up in Thul-Vaishet will pump deadly chemicals into the air – fertiliser cannot be manufactured without polluting the air for miles around. Sulphur dioxide, ammonia and dust will be scattered far and wide. Recently the ruling government stipulated that no fertiliser complex should be located within fifty miles of big cities. But you know how far Rewas is from Bombay – it is only fourteen kilometres as the crow flies. As it is, Bombay is heavily industrialised, crowded and polluted. How much more pollution can we stand? Do you know that in Japan organic

183

mercury was pumped into the sea, it poisoned the fish and the fish poisoned the people who were unlucky enough to eat them …"

Hari strained to listen but the noise of the traffic that was so unfamiliar distracted him. He felt sure the cars and buses were all charging straight at him and if he did not keep a sharp lookout he would be run over. He shifted about uneasily and the men around him bumped into him and talked over his head to each other. The speaker's educated accent was difficult to follow.

"If you are forced to give up farming and fishing, you will have to leave your village and come to Bombay to find work," he was saying. "Look around the city now that you are here: is there room for twenty to fifty thousand more people? Do you think there can be enough jobs here, or houses? See how the poor and unemployed live here. Do you wish to change your life in the country amongst your green paddy fields and coconut groves for the life of beggars on the pavements of the city?"

Hari gave a quiver. He felt certain the bearded gentleman was talking to him, questioning him. His mouth fell open with wonder: how did he know Hari had come here to find work? Hari had told no one, he hardly knew his own mind, but this speaker seemed to know more than even he did about himself. "Who is he?" he asked Mahe who was standing beside him and listening with his mouth open.

"Sayyid – they say his name is Sayyid Ali – something like that," Mahe answered. "Not one of the political leaders. Don't know why they've got hold of him to speak to us."

"He speaks well," Hari said, "very well."

But now he was bowing and climbing down the ladder and a small man in a faded cotton bush-shirt and with wire-rimmed spectacles on his nose was climbing up gingerly to take his place. He was handed the megaphone and began to speak in a squeaky, high-pitched voice. Not only was his voice difficult to follow but Hari could not understand what he was talking about – it was all new and strange. How did these strangers, these city people, know more about Thul and the other fishing villages of the coast than he himself did? He felt more ignorant than he had ever felt in his life.

"You have come from Alibagh," the man began, "a place that means home to you, but to us who work in the meteorological observatory, it means the home of the world-renowned Alibagh geomagnetic observatory, the only one of the type in the world. It was established here in Bombay in 1841, not far from where you are standing, but in 1904 it was shifted to Alibagh because Bombay decided to electrify its tram service which would have created a disturbance in the readings of the observatory …"

"Huh?" grunted Mahe, lifting his turban to scratch his head. "What is all this observe-nobserve he is talking about?"

"Don't know," whispered Hari, trying to hear and learn.

"Now if the fertiliser factory is built near Alibagh, the electric currents and large masses of iron that are brought into the neighbourhood will again vitiate the magnetic observations."

Hari frowned. He understood less and less.

"We supply information to the Survey of India and to the ONGC – the Oil and Natural Gas Commission. It is essential that our functioning is not disturbed or interrupted. It has been uninterrupted since 1846. We cannot allow it to break down now." His voice broke and he gulped and stopped to mop his brow with a large handkerchief. One could see this man was used to working in an office, not to speaking at public meetings. "We – you – all of us should be proud of it. It must be – er – preserved at all cost." Then he gave up the megaphone and stumbled down into the crowd which applauded out of relief that the speech was over. The speaker himself was smiling weakly with relief.

"Who is he? What is he trying to tell us?" everyone was saying to each other.

"Have you seen this observatory in Alibagh?" someone asked. "I don't know where it is."

"Yes, yes, it is a small white house by the sea – I know it," said another sagely. "But I did not know it was so important."

"World–renowned, he said."

"It must be if he says it is."

"Yes, yes, very important," they nodded, impressed.

But another young man, large and hefty, shouted over their heads, "Preserve a rotten old observatory just because it is so old? What about our farms, our crops, our boats? That is what we have come here to see about – not that man's dusty old office or his files or his job."

"Yes, yes that too," an older man placated him. "Here, have a smoke, then we will see about our land and boats."

Now a third man mounted the pedestal. It was their own leader, Adarkar, and so they cheered him loudly although the heat was beginning to wilt them.

His speech soon revived them because it was in their own village dialect and he spoke of the things they knew best. He repeated all he had already talked of before – the richness of their land, the excellence of their crops, of how these must not be given up or destroyed for the sake of the factories, of how they must not be misled by promises of money or jobs, they were unlikely to get any – and everyone nodded and clapped.

"We have come to tell the government we don't want the miserable sums of money they are offering us – our land is too valuable to sell. We are not going to be turned into slaves working in their factories, we have always worked and lived independently and been our own masters. Now let us march to Mantralaya and give our petition to the Chief Minister himself. Let us march, brothers!" and he lifted up his arms and roared the last words.

The roar spread through the whole crowd like a wave surging through it and breaking on the rocks. Suddenly confusion broke out and the crowd began to dissipate and Hari found that the men who had been standing beside him were now drifting away. He hurried first after one group and then after another, wondering where they were going and if he was meant to follow.

Catching the large, hefty young man by his arm, he begged for instructions. "Do we all have to march to Mantralaya now?"

Just then he heard a voice shout over the megaphone: "Friends, make your way back to the Sassoon docks where our boats are waiting for us. Only five farmers will go to Mantralaya with the petition. I am one of them. When we have seen the Chief Minister Sahib, we will join you at the docks and travel back together …"

"There, you've had your answer," said the young man, shaking off Hari's hand from his arm and walking off.

Hari stood watching the crowd fade away down the road. He felt deserted and friendless. None of his friends from the village had come – they were the ones who were sitting happily at home waiting for the fertiliser factory to come up and employ them. He had left them to join the march in order to get away from Thul and get to Bombay, and he knew he did not really belong to the march, he had no fields or fishing boats to fight for, nor did he know any of the marchers who were mainly farmers and fishermen, not the sort of people who would know his landless, boatless, jobless father. He felt now that he belonged neither to one group nor the other. He belonged to no one, nowhere. The others had left him behind. He was alone in Bombay.

Reading for meaning

1 What are Hari's first impressions of Bombay? How are these made vivid to you? *Hint: Look, for example, at the choice of verbs and use of repetition in the first paragraph.*

2 How do you know that Hari has never been in a large city before? *Hint: How does the way of life in Bombay seem strange to Hari?*

3 Why do you think the writer includes the incidents involving:
   a) the bus-driver and the policeman?
   b) the protesting women?

4 Why does the writer include so much detail about the meteorological station? *Hint: What does it tell you both about the speaker and the villagers and their reasons for becoming involved in the protest? Might the writer be using this specific incident to make a more general point about political protests?*

5 Why does Hari feel so alone at the end? What has he decided to do? Why?

Vocabulary and spelling

1 The following words are all used in the text: jostling, mingling, controlling, fearfully, ruling.
   a) What is the root word each one is formed from?
   b) Why is the 'l' doubled in some cases and not in others?

2 When Sayyid is talking about the geomagnetic observatory, he uses the verb 'electrify' with its scientific meaning. How can this verb be used **metaphorically**? *Hint: Think of an actual sentence using the word in this way.*

3 The words 'industrialised' and 'electrify' show two ways of making verbs from the nouns 'industry' and 'electricity'.
   a) List two other verbs which are formed in these same two ways, and a third verb which is formed differently from its linked noun.
   b) Explain in each case how the verb has been formed from the noun, and any spelling rules each case illustrates.

Language variation

This text contains a lot of dialogue in English – English as it is spoken by people in South Asia. Because there are many different native languages spoken in India, and because India was governed by the British until 1947, English is still commonly used there as the language of mass communication and as the legal language of government.

1   Look for examples of:
    a)   expressions, phrases and grammatical constructions which are slightly different from **standard English**
    b)   native words used alongside English.

2   Prepare a brief note about this aspect of language (about 250 words) which could be included in a school edition of this text for readers of your own age.

South Asian English differs from standard UK English in a number of ways.
- The rhythm and stresses in pronunciation are different.
- Some native words are often used mixed in with English (as they are in this text).
- There are grammatical variations, the most common of which is verb forms such as 'I am knowing it', 'she is understanding the answer'.
- Sometimes word order is different, for example 'My all friends are coming'.

Sentences, paragraphs and punctuation

Look again at the first and last paragraphs of this text.
a)   What are the differences between them?
b)   How do these differences show the change in Hari's attitudes and feelings during his brief time in Bombay?

Look closely at:
- what the paragraphs describe
- the structure and length of sentences
- how the sentences within each paragraph are linked
- the use of punctuation
- the use of repetition in vocabulary and grammar.

Writing to imagine, explore and entertain

Write a short narrative which describes someone in a confusing or frightening situation. For example, it could be set:

● in a real place, like Hari's experience in Bombay, or

● within an imaginary setting such as a nightmare.

Concentrate on imagining and exploring the central character's feelings, rather than on dramatic incidents. Use the grid to plan your writing.

Speaking and listening

Think about how the three different speakers in Bombay (Sayyid, the 'small man in a faded cotton bush-shirt' and Adarkar) try to rouse the passions of their listeners. They use techniques such as presenting facts, expressing opinions, quoting dates and statistics, using colourful language, putting questions to the crowd, and so on.

Hold a small group debate.

● Choose a topic – this is known as the **motion**.

● One person will present the case *for* the motion.

● One person will present the case *against* the motion.

● The remaining group members ask questions of both main speakers.

● The group then decide who is the most convincing and persuasive speaker, giving their reasons.

Hint: To prepare for the debate, the main speakers need to make detailed notes about their opening statements. Other group members need to prepare questions and think about how they will give feedback on their persuasiveness to the main speakers. They will need to make notes during the debate.

A **motion** is the topic or subject of a formal debate which leads to a vote. Traditionally, the form of words used in a motion is 'This house believes that …'. Votes at the end of the debate are cast 'For' or 'Against' the motion. Anyone who is undecided can choose not to vote, in which case they are said to 'Abstain'.

The Raffle

In the following short story by V.S. Naipaul, a number of people are in situations which make them feel uncomfortable or angry – but it is a story with a good deal of humour in it, even if it is humour based on the misfortunes of others.

The story is set on the Caribbean island of Trinidad in the recent past.

Reading for meaning

When you have read the text, answer these questions.

1   What is the storyteller's attitude to Mr Hinds in the first nine paragraphs?

2   What signs of the storyteller's naivety are there in this story? Does he change at all? *Hint: Think about his views of the teacher, what he expects from the goat, and how he reacts to the second raffle.*

3   What sort of a person is the storyteller's mother? How do you think she feels towards her son?

4   What do you feel about Mr Hinds by the end of the story?

5   What do you read into the final sentence? *Hint: Why didn't he go to the school any more? Who will have made this decision? Was it the right decision? What might it mean for Vidiadhar's plans for the future?*

The Raffle

They don't pay primary schoolteachers a lot in Trinidad, but they allow them to beat their pupils as much as they want.

Mr Hinds, my teacher, was a big beater. On the shelf below *The Last of England* he kept four or five tamarind rods They are good for beating. They are limber, they sting and they last. There was a tamarind tree in the schoolyard. In his locker Mr Hinds also kept a leather strap soaking in the bucket of water every class had in case of fire.

It wouldn't have been so bad if Mr Hinds hadn't been so young and athletic. At the one school sports I went to I saw him slip off his shining shoes, roll up his trousers neatly to mid-shin and win the Teachers' Hundred Yards, a cigarette between his lips, his tie flapping smartly over his shoulder. It was a wine-coloured tie. Mr Hinds was careful about his dress. That was something else that somehow added to the terror. He wore a brown suit, a cream shirt and the wine-coloured tie.

It was also rumoured that he drank heavily at weekends.

But Mr Hinds had a weak spot. He was poor. We knew he gave those 'private lessons' because he needed the extra money. He gave us private lessons in the ten-minute morning recess. Every boy paid fifty cents for that. If a boy didn't pay, he was kept in all the same and flogged until he paid.

We also knew that Mr Hinds had an allotment in Morvant where he kept some poultry and a few animals.

The other boys sympathised with us – needlessly. Mr Hinds beat us, but I believe we were all a little proud of him.

I say he beat us, but I don't really mean that. For some reason which I could never understand then and can't now, Mr Hinds never beat me. He never made me clean the blackboard. He never made me shine his shoes with the duster. He even called me by my first name, Vidiadhar.

This didn't do me any good with the other boys. At cricket I wasn't allowed to bowl or keep wicket and I always went in at number eleven. My consolation was that I was spending only two terms at the school before going on to Queen's Royal College. I didn't want to go to QRC so much as I wanted to get away from Endeavour (that was the name of the school). Mr Hinds's favour made me feel insecure.

At private lessons one morning Mr Hinds announced that he was going to raffle a goat – a shilling a chance.

He spoke with a straight face and nobody laughed. He made me write out the names of all the boys in the class on two foolscap sheets. Boys who wanted to risk a shilling had to put a tick after their names. Before private lessons ended there was a tick after every name.

I became very unpopular. Some boys didn't believe there was a goat. They all said that if there was a goat, they knew who was going to get it. I hoped they were right. I had long wanted an animal of my own, and the idea of getting milk from my own goat attracted me. I had heard that Mannie Ramjohn, Trinidad's champion miler, trained on goat's milk and nuts.

Next morning I wrote out the names of the boys on slips of paper. Mr Hinds borrowed my cap, put the slips in, took one out, said 'Vidiadhar, is your goat,' and immediately threw all the slips into the wastepaper basket.

At lunch I told my mother, 'I win a goat today.'

193

'What sort of goat?'

'I don't know. I ain't see it.'

She laughed. She didn't believe in the goat, either. But when she finished laughing she said: 'It would be nice, though.'

I was getting not to believe in the goat, too. I was afraid to ask Mr Hinds, but a day or two later he said, 'Vidiadhar, you coming or you ain't coming to get your goat?'

He lived in a tumbledown wooden house in Woodbrook and when I got there I saw him in khaki shorts, vest and blue canvas shoes. He was cleaning his bicycle with a yellow flannel. I was overwhelmed. I had never associated him with such dress and such a menial labour. But his manner was more ironic and dismissing than in the classroom.

He led me to the back of the yard. There *was* a goat. A white one with big horns, tied to a plum tree. The ground around the tree was filthy. The goat looked sullen and sleepy-eyed, as if a little stunned by the smell it had made. Mr Hinds invited me to stroke the goat. I stroked it. He closed his eyes and went on chewing. When I stopped stroking him, he opened his eyes.

Every afternoon at about five an old man drove a donkey-cart through Miguel Street where we lived. The cart was piled with fresh grass tied into neat little bundles, so neat you felt grass wasn't a thing that grew but was made in a factory somewhere. That donkey-cart became important to my mother and me. We were buying five, sometimes six bundles a day, and every bundle cost six cents. The goat didn't change. He still looked sullen and bored. From time to time Mr Hinds asked me with a smile how the goat was getting on, and I said it was getting on fine. But when I asked my mother when we were going to get milk from the goat she told me to stop aggravating her. Then one day she put up a sign:

RAM FOR SERVICE

Apply Within For Terms

and got very angry when I asked her to explain it.

The sign made no difference. We bought the neat bundles of grass, the goat ate, and I saw no milk.

And when I got home one lunch-time I saw no goat.

'Somebody borrow it,' my mother said. She looked happy.

'When it coming back?'

She shrugged her shoulders.

It came back that afternoon. When I turned the corner into Miguel Street I saw it on the pavement outside our house. A man I didn't know was holding it by a rope and making a big row, gesticulating like anything with his free hand. I knew that sort of man. He wasn't going to let hold of the rope until he had said his piece. A lot of people were looking on through curtains.

'But why all-you want to rob poor people so?' he said, shouting. He turned to his audience behind the curtains. 'Look, all-you, just look at this goat!'

The goat limitlessly impassive, chewed slowly, its eyes half-closed.

'But how all you people so advantageous? My brother stupid and he ain't know this goat but I know this goat. Everybody in Trinidad who know about goat know this goat, from Icacos to Mayaro to Toco to Chaguaramas,' he said, naming the four corners of Trinidad. 'Is the most uselessest goat in the whole world. And you charge my brother for this goat? Look, you better give me back my brother money, you hear.'

My mother looked hurt and upset. She went inside and came out with some dollar notes. The man took them and handed over the goat.

That evening my mother said, 'Go and tell your Mr Hinds that I don't want this goat here.'

Mr Hinds didn't look surprised. 'Don't want it, eh?' He thought, and passed a well-trimmed thumb-nail over his

moustache. 'Look, tell you. Going to buy him back. Five dollars.'

I said, 'He eat more than that in grass alone.'

That didn't surprise him either. 'Say six, then.'

I sold. That, I thought, was the end of that.

One Monday afternoon about a month before the end of my last term I announced to my mother, 'That goat raffling again.'

She became alarmed.

At tea on Friday I said casually, 'I win the goat.'

She was expecting it. Before the sun set a man had brought the goat away from Mr Hinds, given my mother some money and taken the goat away.

I hoped Mr Hinds would never ask about the goat. He did though. Not the next week, but the week after that, just before school broke up.

I didn't know what to say.

But a boy called Knolly, a fast bowler and a favourite victim of Mr Hinds, answered for me. 'What goat?' he whispered loudly. 'That goat kill and eat long time.'

Mr Hinds was suddenly furious. 'Is true, Vidiadhar?'

I didn't nod or say anything. The bell rang and saved me.

At lunch I told my mother, 'I don't want to go back to that school.'

She said, 'You must be brave.'

I didn't like the argument, but went.

We had Geography the first period.

'Naipaul,' Mr Hinds said right away, forgetting my first name, 'define a peninsula.'

'Peninsula,' I said, 'a piece of land entirely surrounded by water.'

'Good. Come up here.' He went to the locker and took out the soaked leather strap. Then he fell on me. 'You sell my goat?' Cut. 'You kill my goat?' Cut. 'How you so damn ungrateful?' Cut, cut, cut. 'Is the last time you win anything I raffle.'

It was the last day I went to that school.

Language variation

1 The narrative is in **standard English** but it includes some local words which establish the setting and give local colour. Find some examples of local words and explain how they add to the effectiveness of the story.

2 The dialogue uses some local variations in English typical of **Caribbean English**. Find some **verb** forms which differ from standard English and explain the differences.

Caribbean English covers a wide variety of local differences, as the Caribbean islands stretch for over 1,000 miles off the coasts of North and South America.

• Pronunciation is often different from standard English, especially in the way that syllables are given equal stress in words – you can hear this in much rap music.

• Most islands have their own **dialect** words, some of which are now frequently used in Britain, for example 'calypso', 'dreadlocks', 'rasta'.

• The differences in grammar are most noticeable in verb forms, for example when the **passive** is formed using a **participle** (in this text, 'That goat raffling again' for 'That goat is being raffled again') or by using 'get' as an auxiliary, for example, 'It get break' meaning 'It was broken'.

• Tenses are sometimes used differently too.

Writing to persuade, argue and advise

Imagine that Vidiadhar has been unable to persuade his mother to remove him from Endeavour School. He decides to write a plea to Mr Hinds in which he sets out:

● the reasons for his unhappiness

● how he would like the teacher to behave towards him in the future.

Drama

Prepare and perform the scene when Mr Hinds confronts Vidiadhar, having received his written plea.

Stranger than fiction

A well-known **cliché** suggests that 'life is stranger than fiction'. Made-up stories may seem very unlikely, but sometimes real life can throw up a very odd series of incidents. In the following newspaper report, the insurance company apparently accepted that the events happened just as described!

A **cliché** is a phrase which may once have been original and striking but has become so over-used that it no longer conveys any strength of feeling or opinion. For example, fun is often made of sportspeople who celebrate victory by saying they are 'over the moon' or complain about defeat by saying they are 'sick as a parrot' Both phrases conjure up bizarre images, but have become so familiar that you no longer think about the actual meaning of the words.

As you read

Think about the events in this report. Can you believe they actually happened?

When bike, car, train, horse and dog collide

BY MARK ROWE

It sounds like a script from a sketch for Mr Bean. A driver approaching a level crossing is suddenly confronted with a horse and a pensioner walking his dog. He slams on his brakes. A motorcyclist behind him bumps into the car and is thrown off his bike. The biker lands behind the horse, scaring it so much that it rears up, throwing its rider into a nearby hawthorn hedge.

That is not the end of tale, or even the beginning of the end. It is merely the end of the beginning. The horse bolts. The pensioner rushes to help the fallen horse rider, first tying his Yorkshire terrier to the nearest object, the level crossing barrier.

The train passes through the junction and the warning lights on the level crossing stop flashing. The barrier, to which the terrier has been tethered, slowly starts to rise. At this point the *dramatis personae* must have realised they were helpless agents in the kind of chain reaction one imagines could only be set off by a nuclear scientist.

The dog's owner rushes to rescue the choking animal from the barrier. The dog, agitated and confused, expresses its gratitude by sinking its teeth into the prostrate motorcyclist.

The scene, blending the best of Will Hay and Buster Keaton, was nominated as the most bizarre rental car accident of 1999 by the insurance group Aon Risk Services. Aon declined to release any further details, but said it had paid a sum to the horse rider claiming third party damages for himself and his horse against the car driver, and that the chain of events occurred somewhere in the East Midlands.

"There was a degree of scepticism when the claim first came in, but it stands up," said a spokesman for Aon. "We get some extraordinary claims but, given that no one was actually injured, this was certainly one of the better ones."

Reading for meaning

1 a) What is the point of the reference to Mr Bean?
   b) Who are Will Hay and Buster Keaton? Why are they also mentioned? *Hint: You may need to research this.*

2 Why is the owner of the dog described twice as a pensioner? *Hint: Do newspaper reporters assume certain reactions by readers if they indicate that someone is very old or very young?*

3 a) What does 'dramatis personae' mean?
   b) Where is this phrase usually used? Why is it used here?

4 Why do you think the insurance company refused to release any further details of this incident?

5 Why has the newspaper included an illustration? How is it effective?

Sentence construction and punctuation

1 a) Why has Mark Rowe used the present tense in this report?
   b) Why is there a change of tense at the end of the third paragraph and in the last two paragraphs?

2 Explain what effect the writer creates by using repetition in the first two sentences of the second paragraph. *Hint: How does this relate to the confusion described in the report?*

3 Comment on the phrase 'agitated and confused' in the second sentence of paragraph four.
   a) How would you describe the grammatical function of this phrase?
   b) Why is it punctuated as it is?

4 Why has the writer quoted actual speech at the end of the report?

Writing to inform, explain and describe

Although the incident was certainly bizarre, the situation of different people and various forms of transport waiting at a level crossing is one where there is the potential for odd things to happen.

Imagine that you work for Railtrack. You have been asked to draw up a straightforward set of instructions for the public to prevent incidents like this. Produce a warning notice to be displayed at all level crossings.

Review

What did you particularly enjoy in this chapter?

What did you not like very much?

Was there anything:
- you found difficult to understand?
- you discovered or understood for the first time?

Use this checklist to help you answer these questions and to review the progress you have made.

- **You have read**: two pre-twentieth-century poems; a modern short story and an extract from a novel set in different cultures; an extract from a play written early in the twentieth century, and a short scene from a play by Shakespeare; a newspaper report about an unfortunate series of accidents.

- **You have thought about how writers use**: blank verse, iambic pentameters and other verse forms such as the sonnet; poetic diction and word order, to achieve particular effects; varieties of English spoken in different cultures; genres such as melodrama.

- **You have written to**: imagine, explore and entertain – a newspaper report and a narrative; inform, explain and describe – a magazine article, a piece of ironic writing and a set of instructions; persuade, argue and advise – a plea by a fictional character; analyse, review and comment – a magazine article.

- **To improve your writing you have thought about**: elements of rhetoric; clichés; spelling rules and spelling reform; sentence and paragraph structures.

- **Your speaking and listening work has included**: discussing ideas in pairs and as a class; performing part of a playscript; dramatising and performing a scene from a prose text; choral speaking; small group debate; evaluating your own and others' work.

- **You may have used ICT to**: add to your record of Shakespearian language; research Shelley and produce an information sheet on him; produce a warning notice; spellcheck, and present final drafts of your writing neatly and attractively.

5 Animals

This chapter explores some of the different relationships and attitudes which exist between humans and animals.

When humans were first on the earth, their relationship with the animal kingdom was probably quite different from what we are used to now. There were many more species of wild animals, and many of them were dangerous and threatening to humans. But we know that humans soon began to domesticate animals, not just to have easy access to meat for food, fur for clothes or bones to use as tools, but also for companionship.

So the situation developed that we know today. Many – maybe most – people are animal lovers (or at least, lovers of certain animals), but there are still wild, frightening or dangerous animals in some parts of the world, and some animals are reared only to provide food or clothing or for medical and cosmetic research.

Speaking and listening

1 Think about these questions:

- Do animals have rights? Can humans make whatever use they want of them?

- Is it right to spend time and money protecting endangered species of animals when there are still poor, sick and hungry people in many parts of the world?

- Is it more important to protect animals from pain and suffering, or to use them for testing new drugs or other treatments so that human lives can be saved?

- Should wild animals be put into zoos so that humans can look at them? Should some animals be forced to perform tricks in circuses?

- Is it right to breed animals in captivity simply so that they can be killed to provide food or clothing for humans?

2 In your group, discuss one of the issues.

- Each group will rehearse a brief formal debate with a chairperson, speakers for and against the **motion** and questions from the audience.

- Before each group holds its debate in front of the class, a vote will be taken on the motion.

- At the end of the debate, another vote will be taken to see if people have changed their minds.

- When you are listening to each debate, try to identify features of effective debating. For example, how do the speakers:

  – vary tone, pace, volume?

  – use pauses?

  – tell personal **anecdotes**?

  – refer to statistics and well-publicised cases?

  – use persuasive devices such as questions, humour, sarcasm?

  – use emotional language?

Mythical dragons

There has always been a close relationship between human beings and animals, so animals have often been the subject of legends and travellers' tales. There are many accounts of animals which probably never existed, or at least not quite in the form given to them by imaginative storytellers or writers.

Some of the texts in this chapter are concerned with dragons. Were there ever such creatures? Probably not, although they make an astonishing number of appearances in poems, stories for something which never existed!

Beowulf

Beowulf is one of the earliest English poems which includes an account of a dragon.

Hrothgar, King of the Danes, has built a great banqueting hall known as Heorot. Over a period of time, a monster called Grendel attacks this hall and carries off a number of Danish nobles. Beowulf, the hero, comes over the sea from Sweden to help, and fatally injures Grendel by tearing off his arm. Grendel's mother, a sea-witch, is furious and almost kills Beowulf when he goes to her underwater cave. However, he wins the fight, and cuts off her head – and the head of Grendel, whose body has been kept in the cave by his mother – with a magic sword.

After a number of years, Beowulf becomes King of the Danes and rules for fifty years. But a dragon which has been robbed of some treasure starts to terrorise the land … and Beowulf decides it is time to sort it out.

Beowulf is a poem of more than 3,000 lines dating from about the end of the tenth century. Because real people are referred to in the text, we know that it is set in the early sixth century. Some of the events it records may be based on historical fact, but it is an epic or heroic poem – much of the content is imaginative or far-fetched, intended to praise and popularise the hero, rather like in a James Bond film today. It is written in **Old English**, or **Anglo-Saxon**, and so needs to be read in translation by most people.

The extract which follows is taken from a recent translation of *Beowulf* by the Irish poet, Seamus Heaney.

BEOWULF

The dragon in turmoil.

When the dragon awoke, trouble flared again.
He rippled down the rock, writhing with anger
when he saw the footprints of the prowler who had stolen
too close to his dreaming head.

5 So may a man not marked by fate
easily escape exile and woe
by the grace of God.

              The hoard-guardian
scorched the ground as he scoured and hunted
for the trespasser who had troubled his sleep.

10 Hot and savage, he kept circling and circling
the outside of the mound. No man appeared
in that desert waste, but he worked himself up
by imagining battle; then back in he'd go
in search of the cup, only to discover

15 signs that someone had stumbled upon
the golden treasures. So the guardian of the mound,
the hoard-watcher, waited for the gloaming
with fierce impatience; his pent-up fury
at the loss of the vessel made him long to hit back

20 and lash out in flames. Then, to his delight,
the day waned and he could wait no longer
behind the wall, but hurtled forth
in a fiery blaze. The first to suffer
were the people on the land, but before long

25 it was their treasure-giver who would come to grief.

The dragon began to belch out flames
and burn bright homesteads; there was a hot glow
that scared everyone, for the vile sky-winger
would leave nothing alive in his wake.

30 Everywhere the havoc he wrought was in evidence.
Far and near, the Geat nation
bore the brunt of his brutal assaults
and virulent hate. Then back to the hoard
he would dart before daybreak, to hide in his den.

35 He had swinged the land, swathed it in flame,
in fire and burning, and now he felt secure
in the vaults of his barrow; but his trust was unavailing.

Then Beowulf was given bad news,
a hard truth: his own home,

40 the best of buildings, had been burnt to a cinder,
the throne-room of the Geats. It threw the hero
into deep anguish and darkened his mood:
the wise man thought he must have thwarted
ancient ordinance of the eternal Lord,

45 broken His commandment. His mind was in turmoil,
unaccustomed anxiety and gloom
confused his brain; the fire-dragon
had rased the coastal region and reduced
forts and earthworks to dust and ashes,

50 so the war-king planned and plotted his revenge.
The warrior's protector, prince of the hall-troop,
ordered a marvellous all-iron shield
from his smithy works. He well knew
that linden boards would let him down

*The dragon
wreaks havoc
on the Geats.*

*Beowulf's ominous
feelings about the
dragon*

55 and timber burn. After many trials,
he was destined to face the end of his days
in this mortal world; as was the dragon,
for all his long leasehold on the treasure. …

Beowulf fights the dragon.

Hard by the rock-face that hale veteran,
60 a good man who had gone repeatedly
into combat and danger and come through,
saw a stone arch and a gushing stream
that burst from the barrow, blazing and wafting
a deadly heat, It would be hard to survive
65 unscathed near the hoard, to hold firm
against the dragon in those flaming depths.
Then he gave a shout. The lord of the Geats
unburdened his breast and broke out
in a storm of anger. Under the grey stone
70 his voice challenged and resounded clearly.
Hate was ignited. The hoard-guard recognized
a human voice, the time was over
for peace and parleying. Pouring forth
in a hot battle-fume, the breath of the monster
75 burst from the rock. There was a rumble underground.
Down there in the barrow, Beowulf the warrior
lifted his shield: the outlandish thing
writhed and convulsed and viciously
turned on the king, whose keen-edged sword,
80 an heirloom inherited by ancient right,
was already in his hand. Roused to a fury,
each antagonist struck terror in the other.

Unyielding, the lord of his people loomed
by his tall shield, sure of his ground,
85 while the serpent looped and unleashed itself.
Swaddled in flames, it came gliding and flexing
and racing towards its fate. Yet his shield defended
the renowned leader's life and limb
for a shorter time than he meant it to:
90 that final day was the first time
when Beowulf fought and fate denied him
glory in battle. So the king of the Geats
raised his hand and struck hard
at the enamelled scales, but scarcely cut through:
95 the blade flashed and slashed yet the blow
was far less powerful than the hard-pressed king
had need of at that moment. The mound-keeper
went into a spasm and spouted deadly flames:
when he felt the stroke, battle-fire
100 billowed and spewed. Beowulf was foiled
of a glorious victory. The glittering sword,
infallible before that day,
failed when he unsheathed it, as it never should have.
For the son of Ecgtheow, it was no easy thing
105 to have to give ground like that and go
unwillingly to inhabit another home
in a place beyond; so every man must yield
the leasehold of his days.
                              Before long
the fierce contenders dashed again.
110 The hoard-guard took heart, inhaled and swelled up
and got a new wind; he who had once ruled

Beowulf's sword
fails him.

209

was furled in fire and had to face the worst.

All but one of Beowulf's band withdraw to safety.

No help or backing was to be had then
from his high-born comrades; that hand-picked troop
115 broke ranks and ran for their lives
to the safety of the wood. ...

Inspired again
by the thought of glory, the war-king threw
his whole strength behind a sword-stroke

Another setback

and connected with the skull. And Naegling snapped.
120 Beowulf's ancient iron-grey sword
let him down in the fight. It was never his fortune
to be helped in combat by the cutting edge
of weapons made of iron. When he wielded a sword,
no matter how blooded and hard-edged the blade,
125 his hand was too strong, the stroke he dealt
(I have heard) would ruin it. He could reap no advantage.

The dragon's third onslaught. He draws blood.

Then the bane of that people, the fire-breathing dragon,
was mad to attack for a third time.
When a chance came, he caught the hero
130 in a rush of flame and clamped sharp fangs
into his neck. Beowulf's body
ran wet with his life-blood: it came welling out. ...
Once more the king

Beowulf delivers a fatal wound.

gathered his strength and drew a stabbing knife
135 he carried on his belt, sharpened for battle.
He stuck it deep into the dragon's flank.
Beowulf dealt it a deadly wound. ...
Then the wound
dealt by the ground-burner earlier began
to scald and swell; Beowulf discovered
140 deadly poison suppurating inside him,
surges of nausea, ...
his allotted time

Beowulf senses that he is near death

was drawing to a close, death was very near.

Reading for meaning

1 a) What does the dragon wait for before he attacks the land? When does he return to his lair?

   b) Does this remind you of another legendary monster, one with a human form? *Hint: Think of blood, sharp incisors, necks…!*

2 Why does Beowulf think that the dragon has destroyed his home? *Hint: What does this tell you about part of the poem's purpose?*

3 What does the dragon's lair and the land around it look like? *Hint: You need to look at more than one part of the text to collect all the information you need.*

4 What do lines 104–108 tell us about Beowulf? *Hint: What is happening to him, and what does he think about it?*

5 What is the sequence of events leading to Beowulf's death? What actually kills him?

Old English verse

The poetic form of Beowulf is **blank verse** with four stresses (or main 'beats') to each line. In addition, the Old English poet used the alliterative style, which means that in the original text each line usually contains a threefold alliteration, each falling on one of the strong beats. Heaney sometimes follows this structure exactly, for example in a line (not from the above extract) such as 'and find friendship in the Father's embrace', where the alliteration and three strong beats are on the letter 'f', with the fourth strong beat on the second syllable of 'embrace'.

These conventions are quite difficult to reproduce consistently in translation, and so Seamus Heaney does not stick rigidly to them.

1 Find examples of places where he:
   a) follows the rhythmic and alliterative structure of the original
   b) varies them.

2 What effect does following the original have? Why do you think Heaney may have varied this in particular places? *Hint: Think about how **rhythm** can imitate sense, and how **alliteration** can make connections between words.*

211

> **Old English** or **Anglo-Saxon** is the name given to the language spoken by people inhabiting the area roughly equivalent to modern England until the time of the Norman invasion in 1066. The earliest surviving manuscripts are from around the seventh century, but Old English must have developed long before that, after the departure of the Romans and the arrival of Anglo-Saxon invaders at the start of the fifth century. Old English is very different from modern English, both in vocabulary and grammar.

Language variation

1   One feature of Old English poetry is to use **kennings**, for example 'hoard-guardian' for 'dragon'.

   a)   What other kennings are used to describe the dragon?

   b)   What kennings are used to describe Beowulf?

2   In this extract there are several words which do not have their usual meaning: 'vessel' (line 19), 'barrow' (line 37), 'keen' (line 79). What are the meanings of these words here? What are their more common meanings? Use a dictionary to help you.

3   a)   What are the meanings of 'rased' (line 48) and 'hale' (line 59)?

   b)   Find **homonyms** for both words. What do the homonyms mean?

Make a note of the different spellings and meanings in your spelling and vocabulary book.

> A **kenning** is a device used in Old English poetry, when a compound term is used to describe something without actually naming it, for example 'sea treader' (swan). Kennings were used both for variety and to engage listeners in a mental challenge (as poetry would have been heard, not read, in those days).

Writing to inform, explain and describe

Use the information you have gained about Beowulf to write his **obituary** for *The Anglo-Saxon Times*. Decide what point of view you wish to convey: that he was a great hero, or someone who hung on to power for too long, perhaps?

Writing to explore, imagine and entertain

Imagine that you are one of Beowulf's companions who accompanied him to fight the dragon, but who ran away when they saw how fierce it was.

Describe what happened, and how you felt about it at the time and later, including:

- the reason you agreed to accompany Beowulf in the first place

- a description of the approach to the dragon's lair

- an account of your first sight of the dragon and your reactions

- how you fled and watched Beowulf's struggle from a nearby wood

- what you told others when you returned to the Geats' settlement.

An **obituary** is a newspaper announcement of someone's death. It consists of a brief biography, mentioning the most important events in the subject's life, and details of when, where and how the subject died. If the obituary is of a particularly important or well-known person, it may include comments about them by other people. Although obituaries contain facts about the subject's life, the writer's choice of detail and language usually conveys a positive view of the person.

The Kraken

The next text is a poem by the late **Romantic** poet, Alfred, Lord Tennyson. His poem 'The Kraken' is about another kind of mythical dragon, one that lives deep in the ocean – perhaps like Grendel's mother in Beowulf.

The Kraken

Below the thunders of the upper deep;
Far, far beneath in the abysmal sea,
His ancient, dreamless, uninvaded sleep
The Kraken sleepeth: faintest sunlights flee
About his shadowy sides: above him swell   5
Huge sponges of millennial growth and height;
And far away into the sickly light,
From many a wondrous grot and secret cell
Unnumber'd and enormous polypi
Winnow with giant arms the slumbering green.   10
There hath he lain for ages and will lie
Battening upon huge seaworms in his sleep,
Until the latter fire shall heat the deep;
Then once by man and angels to be seen,
In roaring he shall rise and on the surface die.   15

Reading for meaning

1 In your own words, describe the Kraken's surroundings.

2 What words and phrases tell you that the Kraken has been there for a very long time?

3 What do you learn from this poem about the Kraken's appearance and habits?

4 What is 'the latter fire' mentioned in line 13?

5 What events are described in the last two lines? *Hint: What does the Kraken do? What is the occasion?*

Tennyson's poetic technique

1 What effect is achieved by repeating the word 'far' three times?

2 The structure of this poem is ten lines plus five. What structural device links the two parts?

3 Where are **alliteration** and **onomatopoeia** used to enhance the meaning of the poem?

Vocabulary and spelling

1 a) The word 'abysmal' in line 2 is used with its literal (true) meaning. What is this?
   b) What meaning is more often given to the word nowadays?

2 a) What can you say about the **verb** form 'sleepeth' in line 4? Why do you think the poet has used it?
   b) In what ways is the adjective 'unnumber'd' (line 9) similar? *Hint: Look back at the information about **archaic** language on page 134.*

3 a) From what noun is the adjective 'millennial' derived?
   b) What does the 'mill-' part of these words mean? *Hint: Think of the year 2000 – and the French number* mille!

4 a) 'Polypi' is a plural noun. What does it mean, and what is the singular form?
   b) Do you know any other nouns which follow this spelling rule for forming the plural? *Hint: Think of maths and circles!*

Sentences and punctuation

1 There are only two sentences in this text. Why do you think the first is so long, and the second much shorter? *Hint: Think about what each sentence describes.*

2 Comment on the way in which the first ten lines are punctuated, particularly how colons and semi-colons are used to convey meaning.

Writing to imagine, explore and entertain

It is the day on which the Kraken wakes … Write the story.

Remember to use colourful, dramatic and vivid language in describing the setting and the Kraken itself. This will engage your readers' imagination more effectively than far-fetched events, heroic rescues, and so on.

5.2 Dragons in non-fiction

The Komodo Dragon

Did dragons once roam the earth? Are there still such creatures? Yes – and no! There actually is a reptile known as the Komodo Dragon, which lives on the Indonesian islands to the north of Australia. Of course, it is not a real dragon – it has no wings and it does not breathe fire. Nor does it go around eating people and destroying their homes. But its appearance, size and some of its characteristics give it a dragon-like quality. The following information text tells you all about it.

Reading for meaning

When you have read the text on pages 218–21, answer these questions.

1   What are the features of this lizard which might have led to it being called a dragon? *Hint: Think about its habitats as well as its appearance and habits.*

2   What different reasons are given for the lack of threat to the Komodo Dragon's survival?

3   Why might a Komodo Dragon go to sleep, apart from being tired?

4   How well do Komodo Dragons get on with each other? *Hint: You will need to bring together information from different parts of the text.*

5   If a female Komodo Dragon can lay up to 20 eggs each year, and adults can live for at least 30 years, why are there not more than 3,000 Komodo Dragons?

KOMODO DRAGON

CARD 4

REPTILES & AMPHIBIANS

GROUP 3

CLASS	ORDER	FAMILY	GENUS & SPECIES
Amphibia	*Squamata*	*Varanidae*	*Varanus komodoensis*

The Komodo dragon is the largest true lizard that has ever lived on land, measuring up to 3m in length. It is the top predator on the tiny Indonesian islands where it lives.

CARD 4   GROUP 3   KOMODO DRAGON

KEY FACTS

SIZES
Length: Male 3m, female slightly smaller.
Weight: Adult 100–135kg.

BREEDING
Sexual maturity: 6 years.
Breeding season: June or July.
No. of eggs: Up to 20.
Incubation: 8 months.

LIFESTYLE
Habit: Mostly solitary, but joins with others to breed and feed on carrion.
Diet: Small mammals, pigs, deer and monkeys.
Lifespan: Estimated at 30 years, but 50 years is quite possible.

RELATED SPECIES
The Komodo dragon belongs to the family of monitor lizards which includes other giants such as the 3m-long water monitor as well as the tiny 20cm-long Australian short-tailed monitor.

■ Range of the Komodo dragon

© MXM IMP BV/IMP LTD WILDLIFE FACT FILE

DISTRIBUTION
The Komodo dragon lives exclusively on the Indonesian islands of Komodo, Rintja, Padar, Flores, Gili Mota and Oewada Sami, to the north of Australia.

CONSERVATION
The population is stable at about 3000. Because the Komodo dragon lives mainly on uninhabited islands, it is currently in no great danger from humans.

FEATURES OF THE KOMODO DRAGON

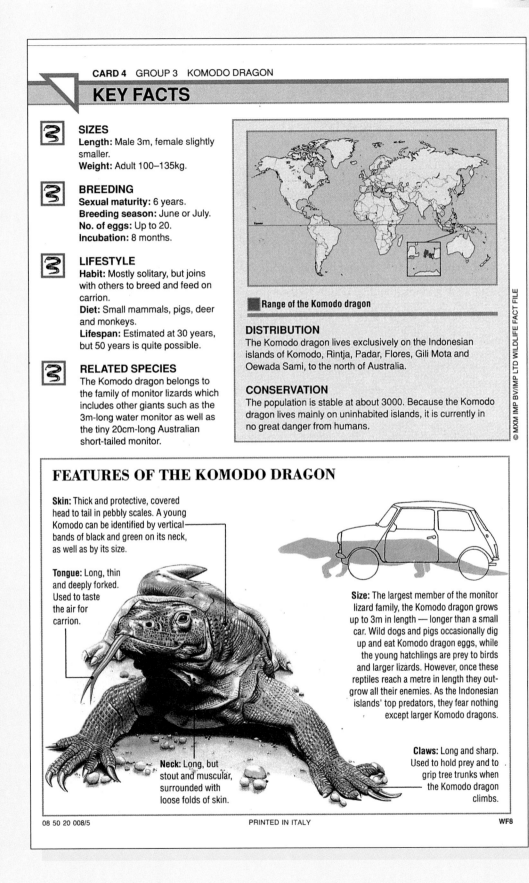

Skin: Thick and protective, covered head to tail in pebbly scales. A young Komodo can be identified by vertical bands of black and green on its neck, as well as by its size.

Tongue: Long, thin and deeply forked. Used to taste the air for carrion.

Size: The largest member of the monitor lizard family, the Komodo dragon grows up to 3m in length — longer than a small car. Wild dogs and pigs occasionally dig up and eat Komodo dragon eggs, while the young hatchlings are prey to birds and larger lizards. However, once these reptiles reach a metre in length they outgrow all their enemies. As the Indonesian islands' top predators, they fear nothing except larger Komodo dragons.

Neck: Long, but stout and muscular, surrounded with loose folds of skin.

Claws: Long and sharp. Used to hold prey and to grip tree trunks when the Komodo dragon climbs.

Armed with the sharp claws and powerful tail of its mythical namesake, the Komodo dragon may not actually breathe fire, but when roused it hisses and flicks its forked tongue menacingly. The dragon's thick and scaly skin is very tough and a dull grey-brown in colour, concealing this fearsome lizard as it lies in wait for prey.

HABITAT

The small Indonesian islands on which the Komodo dragon lives are all quite hilly and sparsely covered in rain forest. The lower areas consist mainly of dry open grassland and fields of wheat, dotted with long-leaved palm trees.

Despite their small size, the islands support a wide range of subtropical plants and animals, including wild pig, monkey and deer.

BEHAVIOUR

The Komodo dragon, in common with most other reptiles, sleeps through the night, resting among tree roots or in sheltered caves or hollows among rocks. As the sun rises and warms its blood, the dragon becomes more active and sets out to search for food.

Despite its great size, the Komodo dragon is an agile creature and moves quickly over the ground. It can outpace a human in thick cover. It sometimes takes to the trees, where it grips the trunk and branches with its strong claws. The Komodo dragon likes water, and swims with forceful strokes of its long tail.

Despite being a solitary creature for most of the time, when two Komodo dragons do meet, they follow an established pecking order, with the smaller dragon giving precedence to a larger and more aggressive one.

BREEDING

The Komodo dragon mates in late June or July. Male dragons often come into conflict at this time as they seek to defend their territory and attract a female. The larger and better placed the territory, the more likely it is that a female will wander into it. When a female does appear, the victorious male licks her head and neck, before clambering on to her back and biting her gently.

Five weeks after mating, the female digs a hole in the warm, moist soil in which to lay her eggs. The number of eggs laid increases with the age and size of the female. After laying the last eggs, the female covers them and leaves

FOOD & HUNTING

The Komodo dragon eats almost anything it can catch and overpower, including other Komodo dragons. Favourite prey includes wild pig, deer and monkey.

Left: The adult Komodo dragon has no enemies except larger members of its own species.

The adult dragon can move quickly only over short distances, so it hunts by ambush. As soon as something edible wanders into its range, the dragon jumps out to seize the prey in its powerful jaws. The Komodo also eats carrion, which it locates by 'tasting' the air with its sensitive tongue.

The young dragon is much more mobile than the adult and hunts actively, feeding on a range of small mammals, young birds and even insects.

The Komodo dragon grips its prey in its claws and jaws. It violently twists its head and body to tear off chunks of flesh, which it then swallows.

them to incubate unattended. She relies on the sun to keep them at the right temperature.

About eight months later, the young dragons hatch and struggle to the surface. Barely 20cm long, the young lizard is now at its most vulnerable. Almost every predator on the islands, from snakes and birds of prey to a larger Komodo dragon, may snap it up.

Those that survive grow quickly. After three years the dragon is nearly 1m long, and more than a match for all predators, except for larger dragons. After five years it reaches a length of about 2m and starts to fill out, becoming thick and heavy-bodied. At about six years, both male and female reach full maturity and are able to breed.

Left: Despite its great size, the Komodo dragon is at ease both on land and in water.

Above: *The Komodo uses its tongue to 'taste' the air.*

Left: *A clear pecking order exists when Komodos meet at a kill, with the larger dragons feeding first and getting the best pickings.*

DID YOU KNOW?

● The adult Komodo dragon can eat most of a deer in one go. It will then sleep for a week to digest it.
● A young dragon emerges from a leathery, goose-sized egg as a small but fully-formed version of its parents.
● The Komodo dragon was officially named in 1912.

Earlier reports had described it simply as a 'land crocodile'.
● The Komodo dragon's tail accounts for only half of its total length.
● As a punishment, criminals were once taken to the Komodo Islands, where they were left to defend themselves against the dragon.

Vocabulary and spelling

1 What sort of words does this text use to suggest the power and strength of the Komodo Dragon?

2 Where and why are **abbreviations** used in this text?

3 a) What is a **homonym** for 'prey'?
   b) What is the difference in meaning between the two words?

   Make a note of the different spellings and meanings in your vocabulary and spelling book.

4 'Mobile' is used as an adjective in this text. What does the word mean when it is used as a noun?

5 The caption to the main photograph describes the Komodo Dragon as 'the largest true lizard that has ever lived on land'. 'Largest' is the **superlative** form of 'large'. What other words are used in this text to compare the Dragon with other creatures?

- To compare the degree of a quality between two objects we use **comparative** adjectives, for example 'The weather in England can be cold but in Russia it can be **colder**.' Most comparatives are formed by adding '-er' to the adjective, but in some cases the word 'more' is used in front of the adjective instead.
- If more than two objects are being compared, the **superlative** is needed, for example 'He is tall, she is taller, but I am the **tallest** in this class.' Superlatives are usually formed by adding '-est' to the adjective, but sometimes 'most' is put in front of the adjective instead.

Writing to analyse, review and comment

How does this text help you understand information about the Komodo Dragon by the way in which it is structured and set out? Consider the following.

- Language – How easy is it to follow? How is technical terminology explained clearly?

- Illustrations – What are the different uses of photographs, drawings and maps?

- Separate boxes – What information is in these, and why?

- Headings and subheadings – How do they help to organise the information?

- Captions – What sort of information do they convey?

- What is the effect of using different typefaces and font sizes? What is the effect of using upper and lower case lettering?

- Colour – How is it used to make the text more eye-catching? Does it help to organise the text in any way?

Write your conclusions in the form of a report to a publisher who is considering this material as the sample for a whole wildlife series aimed at young teenagers.

- Your report should consider the aspects listed above, and any others that occur to you.

- At the end, you should make a clear recommendation about whether you think this sample is good or not, and whether it is aimed at the right market (the people who are going to buy it), with your reasons why.

Writing to inform, explain and describe

Prepare an information sheet about a domestic animal or pet. You may use the Komodo Dragon text to give you some hints about what to include and how to set it out, but remember that this is for a different kind of animal, and so you will need to include different or additional information, for example on how to feed it, how to house it or how to care for the animal if it is sick.

- Your text should fit onto one side of A3 paper, so you will need to plan and edit carefully, to make sure you include the most important information.

- At the bottom of your sheet, acknowledge the sources you have used to gather your information.

- If possible, use a computer to help you present the information attractively.

Zoo Quest for a Dragon

The next text stays with the Komodo Dragon. It is part of an account of an expedition made by the zoologist David Attenborough and some colleagues to study these creatures in their natural habitat. This was the first expedition which set out to track down the Komodo Dragon, and it involved lengthy preparations to ensure that the creatures could be enticed to the spot where the zoologists were waiting for them.

Zoo Quest for a Dragon

The sky was cloudless as we sailed across the bay early the next morning. Haling, seated in the stern of the outrigger canoe, smiled and pointed to the sun, which was already shining fiercely.

"Good," he said. "Much sun; much smell from goats; many buaja."

We landed and set off through the bush as fast as we could. I was impatient to get back to the trap, for it was just possible that a dragon might have entered it during the night. We pushed our way through the undergrowth and emerged on to one of the patches of open savannah. Haling was ahead when suddenly he stopped. "Buaja," he called excitedly. I ran up to him and was just in time to see, fifty yards away on the opposite edge of the savannah, a moving black shape disappear with a rustle into the thorn bushes. We dashed over to the spot. The reptile itself had vanished but it had left signs behind it. The previous day's rain had collected in wide shallow puddles on the savannah, but the morning sun had dried them, leaving smooth sheets of mud, and the dragon we had glimpsed had walked over one of these leaving a perfect set of tracks.

Its feet had sunk into the mud, its claws leaving deep gashes. A shallow furrow, swaying between the pug-marks, showed where the beast had dragged its tail. From the wide spacing of the footprints and the depth to which they had sunk in the mud, we knew that the dragon we had seen had been a large and heavy one. Although our view of the monster had been so short and fragmentary, we were very excited by it; at last we had seen for ourselves the unique and wonderful creature which had been dominating our thoughts for so many months.

We delayed no longer over the tracks, but hurried on towards the trap through the dense bush. As we reached a tall dead tree, which I recognized as being within a very short distance of the stream bed, I was tempted to break into a run, but I checked myself with the thought that to crash noisily through the bush so close to the trap would be a very foolish thing to do, for a dragon might at that very moment be circling the bait. I signalled to Haling and the men to wait. Charles, gripping his camera, Sabran and I picked our way silently through the undergrowth, placing each foot with care and circumspection lest we should tread on a twig and snap it. …

I parted the dangling branches of a bush and peered through across the clear emptiness of the river bed. The trap stood a little below us, a few yards away. Its gate was still hitched high. I felt a wave of disappointment and looked round. There was no sign of a dragon. Cautiously we clambered down to the river bed and examined the trap. Perhaps our trigger had failed to work and the bait had been taken leaving the trap unsprung. Inside, however, the haunch of goat's meat was still hanging, black with flies. The smooth sand around the trap was unmarked except for our own footsteps.

Sabran returned to fetch the boys with the rest of our recording and photographic equipment. Charles began to repair the hides we had erected the day before, and I walked farther up the stream bed to the tree in which we had suspended the major part of our bait. To my delight, I saw that the sand beneath was scuffed and disturbed. Without doubt something had been here earlier trying to snatch the bait. I could understand why, for the stench produced by this mass of rotting meat was incomparably stronger than that given off by the small haunch in the trap. The carcasses were covered by a blanket of handsome orange-yellow butterflies, flexing their wings as they fed on the meat. I reflected sadly that natural history often deals harshly with our romantic illusions about wild life. The most brilliantly beautiful butterflies of the tropical rain forest do not fly in search of appropriately gorgeous blooms, but instead seek a meal from carrion or dung.

As I untied the rope and lowered the carcasses, the butterfly-carpet disintegrated into a flapping cloud, mingling with a swarm of black flies which buzzed around my head. The smell was almost more than I could stand. These big carcasses were obviously more potent magnets than the bait in the trap, and as our primary task was to film the giant lizards, I dragged the meat to a place on the stream bed which was in clear view of the cameras in the hide. Then I drove a stout stake deep into the ground and tied them securely to it, so that the dragons would be unable to pull them away into the bush

and, if they wished to eat, would be compelled to do so within easy range of our lenses. That done, I joined Charles and Sabran behind our screen and settled down to wait.

The sun was shining strongly and

shafts of light struck through the gaps in the branches above us, dappling the sand of the river bed. Although we ourselves were shaded by the bush, it was so hot that sweat poured down us. Charles tied a large handkerchief around his forehead to prevent his perspiration trickling on to the viewfinder of his camera. Haling and the other men sat behind us, chattering among themselves. One of them struck a match and lit a cigarette. Another shifted his seat, and sat on a twig which snapped with a noise that seemed to me to be as loud as a pistol shot. I turned round in irritation with my finger to my lips. They looked surprised but relapsed into silence. Once again I looked anxiously through my peep-hole in the hide, but almost immediately one of the men began talking again. I turned back to them and spoke in an angry whisper.

"Noise no good. Go back to boat. We come to you there when our work is finished."

Looking a little injured, they got to their feet and disappeared through the bush.

There was now little noise. A jungle cock crowed in the distance. Several times a fruit dove, purple-red above and green below, shot with closed wings like a bullet along the clear channel above the stream bed, soundless except for the sudden whistle of its passage through the air. We waited, hardly daring to move, the camera fully wound, spare magazines of film beside us and a battery of lenses ready in the open camera case.

After a quarter of an hour, my position on the ground became extremely uncomfortable. Noiselessly, I shifted my weight on to my hands, and uncrossed my legs. Next to me, Charles crouched by his camera, the long black lens of which projected between the palm leaves of the screen. Sabran squatted on the other side of him. Even from where we sat, we could smell only too strongly the stench of the bait fifteen yards in front of us. This, however, was encouraging for we were relying on this smell to attract the dragons.

We had been sitting in absolute silence for over half an hour when there was a rustling noise immediately behind us. I was irritated; the men must have returned already. Very slowly, so as not to make any noise, I twisted round to tell the boys not to be impatient and to return to the boat. Charles and Sabran remained with their eyes riveted on the bait. I was three-quarters of the way round before I discovered that the noise had not been made by men.

There, facing me, less than four yards away, crouched the dragon.

He was enormous. From the tip of his narrow head to the end of his long keeled tail he measured a full twelve feet. He was so close to us that I could distinguish every beady scale in his hoary black skin, which, seemingly too large for him, hung in long horizontal folds on his flanks and was puckered and wrinkled round his powerful neck. He was standing high on his four bowed legs, his heavy body lifted clear of the ground, his head erect and menacing. The line of his savage mouth curved upwards in a fixed sardonic grin and from between his half-closed jaws an enormous yellow-pink forked tongue slid

in and out. There was nothing between us and him but a few very small seedling trees sprouting from the leaf-covered ground. I nudged Charles, who turned, saw the dragon and nudged Sabran. The three of us sat staring at the monster. He stared back.

It flashed across my mind that at least he was in no position to use his main offensive weapon, his tail.

Further, if he came towards us both Sabran and I were close to trees and I was sure that I would be able to shin up mine very fast if I had to. Charles, sitting in the middle, was not so well placed.

Except for his long tongue, which he unceasingly flicked in and out, the dragon stood immobile, as though cast in gunmetal.

For almost a minute none of us moved or spoke. Then Charles laughed softly.

"You know," he whispered, keeping his eyes fixed warily on the monster, "he has probably been standing there for the last ten minutes watching us just as intently and quietly as we have been watching the bait."

The dragon emitted a heavy sigh and slowly relaxed his legs, splaying them so that his great body sank on to the ground.

"He seems very obliging," I whispered back to Charles. "Why not take his portrait here and now?"

"Can't. The telephoto lens is on the camera and at this distance it would fill the picture with his right nostril."

"Well, let's risk disturbing him and change lens."

Very, very slowly Charles reached in the camera case beside him, took out the stubby wide-angle lens and screwed it into place. He swung the camera round, focused carefully on to the dragon's head and pressed the starting button. The soft whirring of the camera seemed to make an almost deafening noise. The dragon was not in the least concerned but watched us imperiously with his unblinking black eye. It was as though he realized that he was the most powerful beast on Komodo, and that, as king of the island, he feared no other creature. A yellow butterfly fluttered over our heads and settled on his nose. He ignored it. Charles pressed the camera button again and filmed the butterfly as it flapped into the air, circled and settled again on the dragon's nose. …

The smell of the bait drifted over to us and it occurred to me that we were sitting in a direct line between the dragon and the bait which had attracted him here.

Just then I heard a noise from the river bed. I looked behind me and saw a young dragon waddling along the sand towards the bait. It was only about three feet in length and had much brighter markings than the monster close to us. Its tail was banded with dark rings and its forelegs and shoulders were spotted with flecks of dull orange. It walked briskly with a peculiar reptilian gait, twisting its spine sideways and wriggling its hips, savouring the smell of the bait with its long yellow tongue.

Charles tugged at my sleeve, and without speaking pointed up the stream bed to our left. Another enormous lizard was advancing towards the bait. It looked even bigger than the one behind us. We were surrounded by these wonderful creatures.

The dragon behind us recalled our attention by emitting another deep sigh. He flexed his splayed legs and heaved his body off the ground. He took a few steps forward, turned and slowly stalked round us. We followed him with our eyes. He approached the bank and slithered down it. Charles followed him round with the camera until he was able to swing it back into its original position.

The tension snapped and we all dissolved into smothered delighted laughter.

All three reptiles were now feeding in front of us. Savagely they tore at the goat's flesh. The biggest beast seized one of the goat's legs in his jaws. He was so large that I had to remind myself that what he was treating as a single mouthful was in fact the complete leg of a full-grown goat.

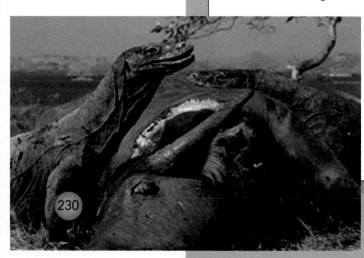

Bracing his feet far apart, he began ripping at the carcass with powerful backward jerks of his entire body. If the bait had not been securely tied to the stake, I was sure he would with ease have dragged the entire carcass away to the forest. Charles filmed feverishly, and soon had exhausted all the film in his magazines.

"What about some still photographs," he whispered.

This was my responsibility, but my camera had not the powerful lenses of the cine camera and I should have to get much closer if I were to obtain good photographs. To do this would risk frightening the beasts. On the other hand, none of the giant lizards would be tempted by the small bait in the trap as long as the carcasses were within their reach, so if we were to capture one, we should have to retrieve the main bait somehow and re-hang it in the tree. It seemed that to try to take their photograph was as good a way of frightening them as any.

Slowly, I straightened up behind the hide and stepped out beside it. I took two cautious steps forward and took a photograph. The dragons continued feeding without so much as a glance in my direction. I took another step forward and another photograph. Soon I had exposed all the film in my camera and was standing nonplussed in the middle of the open river bed within two yards of the monsters. There was nothing else to do but to go back to the hide and reload. Though the dragons seemed preoccupied with their meal, I did not risk turning my back on them as I returned slowly to the hide.

With a new film in my camera I advanced more boldly and did not begin photographing until I was within six feet of them. I inched closer and closer. Eventually, I was standing with my feet touching the forelegs of the goat carcass. I reached inside my pocket and took out a supplementary portrait lens for my camera. The big dragon three feet away withdrew his

head from inside the goat's ribs with a piece of flesh in his mouth. He straightened up, and with a few convulsive snappings of his jaws, he gulped it down. He remained in this position for a few seconds looking squarely at the camera. I knelt and took his photograph. Then he once more lowered his head and began wrenching off another mouthful.

I retreated to Charles and Sabran for a consultation. Obviously, a close approach would not frighten the creatures away. We decided to try noise. The three of us stood up and shouted. The dragons ignored us totally. Only when we rushed together from the hide towards them did they interrupt their meal. The two big ones turned and lumbered up the bank and off into the bush. The little one, however, scuttled straight down the river bed. I chased after it, running as fast as I could, in an attempt to catch it with my hands. It outpaced me, and as it came to a dip in the bank it raced up and disappeared into the undergrowth.

I returned panting and helped Charles and Sabran to hoist the carcasses into a tree twenty yards away from the trap and then once more we waited. I was fearful that having frightened the dragons once they would not return. But I need not have worried; within ten minutes the big one reappeared on the bank opposite us. He thrust his head through the bush and froze immobile. After a few minutes he came to life and descended the bank. For some time he snuffled around the patch of sand where the bait had been lying, protruding his great tongue and tasting the last remnants of the smell in the air. He seemed mystified. He cast around, his head in the air, seeking the meal of which he had been robbed. Then he set off ponderously along the river bed, but to our dismay walked straight past our trap towards the suspended bait. As he approached it, we realized that we had not tied it sufficiently high, for the great creature reared up on its hind legs, using its enormous muscular tail as a counterbalance, and with a downward sweep of his foreleg snatched down a tangle of the goat's innards. He wolfed it immediately, but the end of a long rope of intestine hung down from the angle of his jaw. This displeased him and for a few minutes he tried to paw it off, but without success.

He lumbered along the stream bed, back towards the trap, shaking his head angrily. As he reached a large boulder, he stopped, rasped his scaly cheek against it and at last wiped his jaws clean. Now he was near the trap. The smell of the bait inside filtered into his nostrils and he turned aside from his path to investigate. Sensing accurately the direction from which the smell came, he moved directly to the closed end of the trap and with savage impatient swipes of his forelegs he ripped aside the palm-leaf shroud, exposing the wooden bars. He forced his blunt snout between two of the poles and heaved with his powerful neck. To our relief, the lianas binding the bars together held firm. Baulked, he at last approached the door. With maddening caution, he looked inside. He took three steps forward. All we could see of him was his hindlegs and his enormous tail. For an interminable time he made no movement. At last he went further inside and disappeared entirely from view. Suddenly there was a click, the trigger rope flew loose and the gate thudded down, burying its sharpened stakes deep into the sand.

Exultantly we ran forward. We grabbed boulders and piled them against the trap door. The dragon peered at us superciliously, flicking his forked tongue through the bars. We could hardly believe that we had achieved the objective of our four months' trip, that in spite of all our difficulties we had at last succeeded in catching a specimen of the largest lizard in the world. We sat on the sand looking at our prize and smiling breathlessly at one another.

Reading for meaning

1 How can you work out what the foreign word 'buaja' (used in paragraphs 2 and 3) must mean?

2 Why do you think the writer has included the last two sentences of paragraph seven ('I reflected sadly …')?

3 When the writer sends some of the men back to the boat, why does he speak to them using non-**standard English**? *Hint: Look at how the men speak to him. What does this suggest about their knowledge and use of English?*

4 What clues are there in this text that the writer and his companions are nervous of the Komodo Dragons?

5 What surprises them most about the Komodo Dragons? *Hint: A full answer should include references to the animals' behaviour as well as their appearance.*

Vocabulary

1 How are the verbs in the third, fourth and fifth paragraphs chosen to give you a clear idea of how the group moves towards the trap by the river, and what their feelings are at this time?

2 In the paragraph beginning 'Very, very slowly Charles reached in the camera case …', the dragon is described as 'king of the island'.
   a) What adverb used in the same paragraph echoes this description?
   b) What other members of that word family do you know?

3 Although the writer is impressed by the dragons, he conveys some distaste at their feeding habits. Pick out some of the words and phrases used to convey this feeling. How do they make you feel?

Sentences, paragraphs and punctuation

1 How does the writer use paragraphing to emphasise the drama of the moment when he first sees one of the dragons?

2 Look again at the paragraph beginning 'This was my responsibility …'. The opening sentence of this paragraph is written in very formal **standard English**. Comment on these features, and on how the sentence might be written less formally.

3 Look again at the penultimate paragraph beginning 'He lumbered along …'. Comment on how the writer has used different sentence structures and lengths to convey the excitement of the moment as well as to simply describe what was happening.

Comparison of texts

1 What is there in this text which confirms what you already knew about Komodo Dragons from the previous information text?

2 What new information about the Dragon do you learn from this text? Is it important information for someone who wants to know about them?

3 a) Which text about the Komodo Dragon did you prefer reading? Why?

   b) For what different kinds of readers would these two texts be suitable?

Writing to persuade, argue and advise

You have just read David Attenborough's account of capturing a Komodo Dragon. Write a letter to him, in which you tell him how much you enjoyed reading his book, but express your concern at his wanting to keep one of the animals in captivity.

Remember that this is a formal letter to someone you do not know. It should be polite, but you must make your feelings clear.

Donkeys then and now

Donkeys in literature have almost always been presented as unappealing creatures, and to call someone a donkey is still regarded as a hurtful insult.

This section includes some texts which present the conventional view of donkeys, and others which may make you think more about the animal's special qualities.

The Ass Carrying Salt

This very short text is one of Aesop's famous *Fables*. Aesop probably lived in the middle of the sixth century BC. He wrote about donkeys (or asses, as he tended to call them) in a number of fables. In this example, the conventional view of the unintelligent donkey is used to warn people that trying to be too cunning or clever may have the opposite result from what was intended.

Reading for meaning

1 Why do you think Aesop chose to use a donkey as the main character in this fable? *Hint: What were donkeys used for in ancient times?*

2 Why do you think the writer has used the word 'perished' to end the text rather than 'died'?

3 What hints are there that it was probably a spoken text before it was ever written down? *Hint: Think about length, content and style.*

4 Could you draw a different moral from this fable? What could it be?

A **fable** is a short **narrative** intended to make a moral point or give a moral lesson. The 'characters' are often animals which are given human qualities. The most famous set of fables is that written by Aesop. Each of Aesop's *Fables* ends with the moral or message clearly stated.

The Ass Carrying Salt

An ass with a load of salt was crossing a stream. He slipped and fell into the water. Then the salt dissolved, and when he got up his load was lighter than before, so he was delighted. Another time, when he arrived at the bank of a stream with a load of sponges, he thought that if he fell into the water again when he got up the load would be lighter. So he slipped on purpose. But, of course, the sponges swelled up with the water and the ass was unable to get up again, so he drowned and perished.

Thus it is sometimes that people don't suspect that it is their own tricks which land them in disaster.

Sentence structure and punctuation

1   This fable sets out a logical process or sequence of events. Which words ensure **cohesion** within sentences and coherence across the whole text? *Hint: The moral is also a part of the text.*

> **Cohesion** refers to the way in which a sentence is logically constructed. For example, in the third sentence of the fable, the words 'then', 'when' and 'so' guide you through the sequence, causes and effects of what happened.

2   The penultimate sentence is very much shorter than any others in the text. What effect does this have on the reader?

3   Why are there commas before and after 'of course'?

237

Addicted

Tony Adams has been a well-known member of the Arsenal football team for a number of years. He grew up in Essex, joined Arsenal as a teenager, and has been with the club ever since.

Despite his success as a footballer, his life has not always been happy either professionally or personally. He became an alcoholic, and was imprisoned on a drink-driving charge. Many spectators questioned his skill as a player, and quite early in his career this led to Adams being called a donkey, so that followers of other teams began to chant 'ee-aw' at him when he played against them. Tony Adams decided to write an honest account of his early life, which he called *Addicted*, and the following extracts describe some of the taunting he endured.

The first piece describes the start of the 1988–9 football season. During the summer of 1988, England lost all three games in the opening round of the European Championship Finals. Tony Adams, although a new and young member of the national team, had taken a lot of criticism for the defeats. He felt this was unfair, but once the preparations for the new season in England were under way, things seemed to be getting better.

Addicted

The omens were good pre-season when we won the Wembley International tournament by beating Tottenham and Bayern Munich and in October we lifted the Football League's Centenary Trophy by beating Manchester United at Villa Park. It was strange how at that time, when I was playing well and Arsenal were getting up a head of steam, my England career stalled. We had only drawn 1–1 in Saudi Arabia and although I scored our goal, I was blamed for the one we conceded despite the fact I was up for a corner at the time. That included a public admonishment by the England manager Bobby Robson, although to be fair I think he was going through his own testing time with the media. Anyway, I would be dropped after that game. I was reasonably philosophical about it; if that was the way the wind was blowing at international level, I was going to concentrate my efforts with Arsenal.

What with that result coming on top of the summer's misery, I was being considered a scapegoat for the ills of the English game. I didn't have enough pace and I couldn't bring the ball out of defence – that old argument against the English defender. I seemed to be dubbed as the archetype. One of the chants popular on the terraces at that time was the donkey 'ee-aw' braying aimed by opposing fans at defenders if they misplaced a pass or cleared the ball into touch and I was a target, along with a few others. I think I first heard it at West Ham in the beginning of October, in a game that we won 4–1, then at Derby County's old Baseball Ground the following month. It was always at its loudest at the confined stadiums where you could hear everything.

Then, the following spring – the day after April Fool's Day, in fact – we played at Manchester United and drew 1–1, with me scoring at both ends. After the coach journey back, I stayed the night at Paul Merson's near St Albans.

Paul had the *Daily Mirror* delivered and I woke up to a picture of me on its back page with a pair of donkey's ears drawn on. I was really hurt. After that it just got worse and a month later in our next away match at Middlesbrough's old Ayresome Park ground, so many carrots were thrown at me that I could have opened a fruit and veg stall. One caught me right on the ear, which was really swollen after the game.

That stung physically and emotionally. I dismissed it as all part of the job and used it to focus on my game. Publicly it motivated me, and I used to enjoy winning games away from Highbury – and we were becoming experts at digging in and winning away games – so I could get one over the opposing fans giving out the abuse. In fact, I used to say to the lads that they had chosen the right – or wrong – person to pick on because I was bigger and better than that and I could take it. Kicking the ball into touch? Well, it couldn't be in the back of my net then, could it? That was my attitude.

Despite the criticisms, Tony Adams held his place in the Arsenal and England teams for the next ten years. By the latter part of the 1997–8 season, Arsenal have made it to the quarter-finals of the FA Cup. The game, against London rivals West Ham United, ends in a draw after extra time and a penalty shoot-out is needed to decide the winners. The teams are still level after five penalty-kicks each, and so it goes to 'sudden death'.

Now here we were, in an FA Cup quarter-final and the two teams involved in a penalty shoot-out. Now here I was, the first five penalties not having settled it, finding that I had to shoulder the responsibility for taking one. I didn't much like the idea but felt I should take courage with others unwilling to risk it.

I just wanted to get it over with as quickly as possible. I put the ball on the spot and ran up hastily. I didn't know where I was going to put the ball, but then I thought that the goalkeeper wouldn't either. As I began my run-up I wondered what I had done. All the fans were braying 'ee-aw' at me, at the ground where I first recall the chant, and I thought that this could be the biggest mistake of my life. Before I knew it, I had stroked the ball and it had dribbled home. It was a completely pathetic penalty, I admit, and I had this illogical idea of following it in to knock home any rebound. As I ran back to the centre circle I exhaled deeply and smiled the smile of a relieved man.

Reading for meaning

1 Why was Tony Adams dropped from the England team in 1988? *Hint: There is more than one possible reason.* What was his reaction to this?

2 a) Why was the 'ee-aw' chanting worse at some grounds than at others?
   b) What effect did the chanting have on Tony Adams?

3 Why is Tony Adams so relieved at the end of the second extract?

4 What links these two extracts?

5 From the evidence of these two extracts, what sort of person is Tony Adams? *Hint: Look for the meaning behind the words. What adjectives would you use to describe him? Why? Is he always good at describing his own feelings or reactions accurately?*

Language variation

1 In the first extract, what features of **informal** English are used to create the effect of the writer speaking directly to you? *Hint: Look, for example, at* **contractions**, **abbreviations** *and vocabulary.*

Abbreviations or **contractions** describe words which have been shortened.
- Some of these are so common that we hardly think about them as abbreviations at all, for example, 'fridge' (shortened from 'refrigerator') or 'bus' (shortened from 'omnibus').
- Some abbreviations may be acronyms, where the initial letters of words in a phrase are used to make a 'word' or recognisable set of letters themselves, for example EU (European Union).
- Contractions is the term usually applied to two words being shortened to one, with missing letters indicated by an apostrophe, for example 'don't', 'can't'.

2 In the first extract, find examples of **formal**, written language which would not sound natural if spoken. Why do you think the writer has used these?

3 a) In the second extract, how many words or phrases are used which have a special meaning in the context of football?

   b) What meanings might they have in other contexts?

   c) Arrange and present this information helpfully for someone who has no knowledge of football terminology.

Sentences, paragraphs and punctuation

1 Look at the first paragraph of the first extract. In the sentence beginning 'We had only drawn 1-1 in Saudi Arabia', what is the effect of the words 'although' and 'despite'? *Hint: What do they tell us about what happened in the game and how Tony Adams felt about what happened afterwards?*

2 a) At the start of the third paragraph in the first extract, why do you think the writer has inserted the words 'the day after April Fool's Day, in fact'?

   b) Why is there a dash before and after these words?

3 Why do you think the writer has used two rhetorical questions at the end of the first extract?

4 a) What effect does the writer create by using the repetitive pattern in the first two sentences of the second extract? *Hint: How does the device help to convey Tony Adams' feelings at this moment?*

   b) Where else is repetition used in this extract? What effect does it have?

Writing to inform, explain and describe

Write a few paragraphs about an incident or episode in your life when you felt you were treated unfairly.

● Think about the Tony Adams text, and concentrate on communicating your feelings about the situation and people involved, rather than a detailed account of the events or circumstances.

● Think about ways of making your experience vivid for the reader, for example through your choice of vocabulary and use of sentence and paragraph structures.

Travels with a Donkey

Robert Louis Stevenson is a writer you may know through his adventure stories such as *Treasure Island* or *Kidnapped*, the horror story *The Strange Case of Dr Jekyll and Mr Hyde*, or his poetry collection, *A Child's Garden of Verses*. He was born in Edinburgh in 1850, and suffered from chest infections from an early age. This did not prevent him travelling widely, even as far as the Pacific Islands – he died in Samoa, aged only 44.

In September 1878, Stevenson set off on a walking tour of the Cevennes region of France. He kept a daily diary, from which he took the material for his book *Travels with a Donkey*. As you will see, Stevenson was not always kind to Modestine, but developed a genuine affection for her.

The extract begins with Stevenson's decision to obtain an animal to carry his luggage. It then describes part of his first day on the road with the donkey, and finally gives an account of Stevenson's parting from Modestine.

Travels with a Donkey

I could not carry this huge package on my own, merely human, shoulders. It remained to choose a beast of burden. Now, a horse is a fine lady among animals, flighty, timid, delicate in eating, of tender health; he is too valuable and too restive to be left alone, so that you are chained to your brute as to a fellow galley-slave; a dangerous road puts him out of his wits; in short, he's an uncertain and exacting ally, and adds thirty-fold to the troubles of the voyager. What I required was something cheap and small and hardy, and of a stolid and peaceful temper; and all these requisites pointed to a donkey.

There dwelt an old man in Monastier, of rather unsound intellect according to some, much followed by street-boys, and known to fame as Father Adam. Father Adam had a cart, and to draw the cart a diminutive she-ass, not much bigger than a dog, the colour of a mouse, with a kindly eye and a determined under-jaw. There was something neat and high-bred, a quakerish elegance, about the rogue that hit my fancy on the spot. Our first interview was in Monastier market-place. To prove her good temper, one child after another was set upon her back to ride, and one after another went head over heels into the air; until a want of confidence began to reign in youthful bosoms, and the experiment was discontinued from a dearth of subjects. I was already backed by a deputation of my friends; but as if this were not enough, all the buyers and sellers came round and helped me in the bargain; and the ass and I and Father Adam were the centre of a hubbub for near half an hour. At length, she passed into my service for the consideration of sixty-five francs and a glass of brandy. The sack had already cost eighty francs and two glasses of beer; so that Modestine, as I instantly baptised her, was upon all accounts the cheaper article. …

I had a last interview with Father Adam in a billiard-room at the witching hour of dawn, when I administered the brandy. He

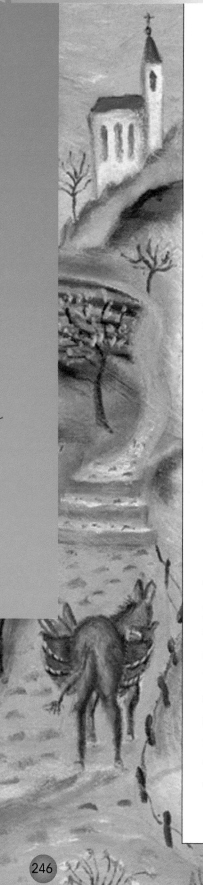

professed himself greatly touched by the separation, and declared he had often bought white bread for the donkey when he had been content with black bread for himself; but this, according to the best authorities, must have been a flight of fancy. He had a name in the village for brutally misusing the ass; yet it is certain that he shed a tear, and the tear made a clean mark down one cheek. …

On the day of my departure I was up a little after five; by six we began to load the donkey; and ten minutes after, my hopes were in the dust. The pad would not stay on Modestine's back for half a moment. I returned it to its maker, with whom I had so contumelious a passage that the street outside was crowded from wall to wall with gossips looking on and listening. …

I had a common donkey pack-saddle – a *barde*, as they call it – fitted upon Modestine; and once more loaded her with my effects. The doubled sack, my pilot-coat (for it was warm, and I was to walk in my waistcoat), a great bar of black bread, and an open basket containing the white bread, the mutton, and the bottles, were all corded together in a very elaborate system of knots, and I looked on the result with fatuous content. …

The bell of Monastier was just striking nine as I got quit of these preliminary troubles and descended the hill through the common. As long as I was within sight of the windows, a secret shame and the fear of some laughable defeat withheld me from tampering with Modestine. She tripped along upon her four small hoofs with a sober daintiness of gait; from time to time she shook her ears or her tail; and she looked so small under the bundle that my mind misgave me. We got across the ford without difficulty – there was no doubt about the matter, she was docility itself – and once on the other bank, where the road begins to mount through pine-woods, I took in my right hand the unhallowed staff, and with a quaking spirit applied it to the donkey. Modestine brisked up her pace for perhaps three steps, and then relapsed into her former minuet. Another application had the same effect, and so with the third. I am worthy the name of an Englishman, and it goes against my conscience to lay my hand rudely on a female. I desisted, and looked her all over from head to foot; the poor brute's knees were trembling and her breathing was distressed; it was plain that she could go no faster on a hill. God forbid, thought I, that I should brutalise this innocent creature; let her go at her own pace, and let me patiently follow.

What that pace was, there is no word mean enough to describe; it was something as much slower than a walk as a walk is slower than a run; it kept me hanging on each foot for an incredible length of time; in five minutes it exhausted the spirit and set up a fever in all the muscles of the leg. And yet I had to keep close at hand and measure my advance exactly upon hers; for if I dropped a few yards into the rear, or went on a few yards ahead, Modestine came instantly to a halt and began to browse. The thought that this was to last from here to Alais nearly broke my heart. Of all conceivable journeys, this promised to be the most tedious. I tried to tell myself it was a lovely day; I tried to charm my foreboding spirit with tobacco; but I had a vision ever present to me of the long, long roads, up hill and down dale, and a pair of figures ever infinitesimally moving, foot by foot, a yard to the minute, and, like things enchanted in a nightmare, approaching no nearer to the goal.

In the meantime there came up behind us a tall peasant, perhaps forty years of age, of an ironical snuffy countenance, and arrayed in the green tail-coat of the country. He overtook us hand over hand, and stopped to consider our pitiful advance.

'Your donkey,' says he, 'is very old?'

I told him, I believed not.

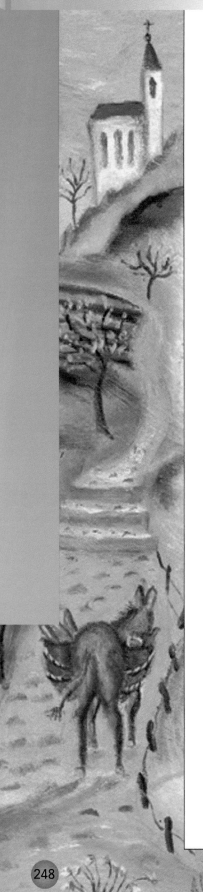

Then, he supposed, we had come far.

I told him, we had but newly left Monastier.

'*Et vous marchez comme ça!*' cried he; and, throwing back his head, he laughed long and heartily. I watched him, half prepared to feel offended, until he had satisfied his mirth; and then, 'You must have no pity on these animals,' said he; and, plucking a switch out of a thicket, he began to lace Modestine about the stern-works, uttering a cry. The rogue pricked up her ears and broke into a good round pace, which she kept up without flagging, and without exhibiting the least symptom of distress, as long as the peasant kept beside us. Her former panting and shaking had been, I regret to say, a piece of comedy.

My *deus ex machina*, before he left me, supplied some excellent, if inhumane, advice; presented me with the switch, which he declared she would feel more tenderly than my cane; and finally taught me the true cry of donkey-drivers, 'Proot!' …

I hurried over my mid-day meal, and was early forth again. But, alas, as we climbed the interminable hill upon the other side, 'Proot!' seemed to have lost its virtue. I prooted like a lion. I prooted mellifluously like a sucking-dove; but Modestine would be neither softened nor intimidated. She held doggedly to her pace; nothing but a blow would move her, and that only for a second. I must follow at her heels, incessantly belabouring. A moment's pause in this ignoble toil, and she relapsed into her own private gait. I think I never heard of anyone in as mean a situation. I must reach the lake of Bouchet, where I meant to camp, before sun-down, and, to have even a hope of this, I must instantly maltreat this uncomplaining animal. The sound of my own blows sickened me. Once, when I looked at her, she had a faint resemblance to a lady of my acquaintance who formerly loaded me with kindness; and this increased my horror of my cruelty. …

A little out of the village, Modestine, filled with the demon, set her heart upon a by-road, and positively refused to leave it. I dropped all my bundles, and, I am ashamed to say, struck the poor sinner twice across the face. It was pitiful to see her lift up her head with shut eyes, as if waiting for another blow. I came very near crying; but I did a wiser thing than that, and sat squarely down by the roadside to consider my situation under the cheerful influence of tobacco and a nip of brandy. Modestine, in the meanwhile, munched some black bread with a contrite hypocritical air. It was plain that I must make a sacrifice to the gods of shipwreck. I threw away the empty bottle destined to carry milk; I threw away my own white bread, and, disdaining to act by general average, kept the black bread for Modestine; lastly, I threw away the cold leg of mutton and the egg-whisk, although this last was dear to my heart. Thus I found room for everything in the basket, and even stowed the boating-coat on the top. By means of an end of cord I slung it under one arm; and although the cord cut my shoulder, and the jacket hung almost to the ground, it was with a heart greatly lightened that I set forth again.

I had now an arm free to thrash Modestine, and cruelly I chastised her. If I were to reach the lakeside before dark, she must bestir her little shanks to some tune. Already the sun had gone down into a windy-looking mist; and although there were still a few streaks of gold far off to the east on the hills and the black fir-woods, all was cold and grey about our onward path. An infinity of little country by-roads led hither and thither among the fields. It was the most pointless labyrinth. I could see my destination overhead, or rather the peak that dominates it; but choose as I pleased, the roads always ended by turning away from it, and sneaking back towards the valley, or northward along the margin of the hills. The failing light, the waning colour, the naked, unhomely, stony country through which I was travelling, threw me into some despondency. I promise you, the stick was not idle; I think every decent step that Modestine took must have cost me at least two emphatic blows. …

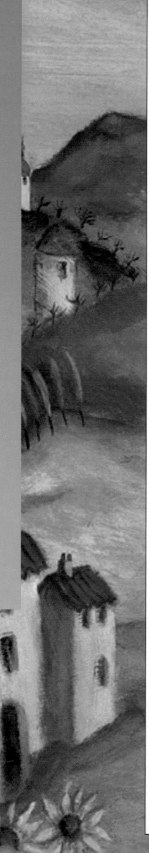

Farewell, Modestine!

On examination, on the morning of 4th October, Modestine was pronounced unfit for travel. She would need at least two days' repose, according to the ostler; but I was now eager to reach Alais for my letters; and, being in a civilised country of stage-coaches, I determined to sell my lady friend and be off by the diligence that afternoon. Our yesterday's march, with the testimony of the driver who had pursued us up the long hill of St Pierre, spread a favourable notion of my donkey's capabilities. Intending purchasers were aware of an unrivalled opportunity. Before ten I had an offer of twenty-five francs; and before noon, after a desperate engagement, I sold her, saddle and all, for five-and-thirty. The pecuniary gain is not obvious, but I had bought freedom into the bargain. …

It was not until I was fairly seated by the driver, and rattling through a rocky valley with dwarf olives, that I became aware of my bereavement. I had lost Modestine. Up to that moment I had thought I hated her; but now she was gone,

> And oh!
> The difference to me!

For twelve days we had been fast companions; we had travelled upwards of a hundred and twenty miles, crossed several respectable ridges, and jogged along with our six legs by many a rocky and many a boggy by-road. After the first day, although sometimes I was hurt and distant in manner, I still kept my patience; and as for her, poor soul! she had come to regard me as a god. She loved to eat out of my hand. She was patient, elegant in form, the colour of an ideal mouse, and inimitably small. Her faults were those of her race and sex; her virtues were her own. Farewell, and if for ever –

Father Adam wept when he sold her to me; after I had sold her in my turn, I was tempted to follow his example; and being alone with a stage-driver and four or five agreeable young men, I did not hesitate to yield to my emotion.

Reading for meaning

1 What sort of a person is Father Adam, and how does the writer convey this picture of him? *Hint: How much is openly stated, and what does Stevenson leave you to work out for yourself?*

2 How does Stevenson create **humour** in his description of buying and loading the donkey? *Hint: Think about the situations he describes and the language he uses to describe them.*

3 How does Stevenson show his mixed feelings about the way he treats Modestine during his first day's walk?

4 In the paragraph beginning 'I had now an arm free ...', Stevenson makes the countryside seem unattractive and unfriendly. How does his choice of words and **imagery** create this feeling?

5 Why is Stevenson so upset to part from Modestine? Why does he allow himself to give in to his emotions?

Humour in texts can be created in many ways.

• A writer may include a joke, or may use language in ways that amuse you, such as punning, for example when Shakespeare has the dying Mercutio say 'Send for me tomorrow and you shall find me a grave man', the word 'grave' means both 'serious' and 'in a grave'.

• Characters may be amusing because of what they say or do, or the exaggerated language a writer uses to describe them and their actions.

• Situations may be humorous for reasons such as **irony** (when you, the reader, know something the characters don't know), or 'slapstick', when things keep going wrong.

Vocabulary and spelling

1 Look at the sentence in the second paragraph which begins 'To prove her good temper ...'.
   a) What does the word 'want' mean here?
   b) Do you know any other examples where this meaning of the word is still in use?

2 a) Find out the meaning of the following words used in this text:
      contumelious; unhallowed; snuffy; nickering; ostler.

   b) Which of them might still be used today? In what context and for
       what effect?

3 The word 'diligence' is used nowadays to mean 'care' or
   'thoroughness'.

   a) What is its meaning in the opening paragraph of the last section
       of this text?

   b) How do you think the word came to have two such different
       meanings? *Hint: You will need to research using an* **etymological**
       dictionary and possibly other sources.

4 The writer uses the adjective 'conceivable' in this text.
   a) What are some other members of this word family?
   b) What spelling rules do they illustrate?

Speaking and listening

Several aspects of this text suggest that it is not set in the present day, or
in England. Discuss what evidence there is, and prepare a brief group
presentation to the class on the social, cultural and historical setting of
Travels with a Donkey.

You should consider aspects such as:

- details of everyday life described in the text, for example food,
  transport, occupations, etc.

- attitudes towards animals

- attitudes towards women

- the emotions described

- the language used.

Drama

In your group, choose one of the incidents mentioned in the text and
improvise a scene based on it. You may stick very closely to the original,
or you may change it to a different (for example, modern) setting in
order to bring out the same point.

Sentences, paragraphs and punctuation

1 a) Explain the use of semi-colons in the second sentence of the text, which begins 'Now, a horse is a fine lady …'.

   b) What comment would you make about Stevenson's general use of the semi-colon?

2 In the same sentence, why might you consider the writer's use of the pronouns 'he' and 'him' as peculiar? What is an explanation for this usage?

3 The sentence which begins the second paragraph has an unusual structure. Why do you think it may have been written in this way? *Hint: Does the opening remind you of any particular kind of writing? What effect could Stevenson be trying to create?*

4 The last sentence of the fifth paragraph ('I went forth from the stable-door …') is also intended to remind you of a particular style of writing or a particular book. What is this? What is the writer's purpose here?

5 Comment on the position and meaning of the adverb 'cruelly' in the sentence 'I had now an arm free to thrash Modestine, and cruelly I chastised her.'

Writing to analyse, review and comment

Imagine that you are the Literary Editor of a daily newspaper in the late 1870s. You have been sent the above extracts from R.L. Stevenson's *Travels with a Donkey* for review. Stevenson is not yet a well-known author, and this is the first piece of his writing that you have read.

Write a review of the extracts for your readers.

- Analyse the strengths and weaknesses of the work as you see them.

- Comment on who you think might enjoy it, what you think the author's prospects are, and so on.

Remember your earlier work on the social, cultural and historical setting of the book – your audience is not a modern one!

The Donkey

This text is not only about a donkey, but represents the donkey's point of view. It is a poem by G.K. Chesterton, a writer and artist who is probably best remembered today for his stories about Father Brown, a fictional priest who is also an amateur detective. Most of Chesterton's writing was completed in the early part of the twentieth century; in his later years he was converted to Roman Catholicism and wrote mostly about religious subjects, an interest which can be seen in this poem.

THE DONKEY

When fishes flew and forests walked,
  And figs grew upon thorn,
Some moment when the moon was blood
  Then surely I was born;

With monstrous head and sickening cry   5
  And ears like errant wings,
The devil's walking parody
  On all four-footed things.

The tattered outlaw of the earth,
  Of ancient crooked will;   10
Starve, scourge, deride me: I am dumb,
  I keep my secret still.

Fools! For I also had my hour;
  One far fierce hour and sweet:
There was a shout about my ears,   15
  And palms before my feet.

Reading for meaning

1 What is the situation described in first stanza?

2 What does the donkey say in stanza 2 about its appearance?

3 What is the 'ancient crooked will' in stanza 3?

4 What is the secret the donkey refers to in stanza 3?

5 What is the event described in stanza 4?

Chesterton's poetic technique

1 G.K. Chesterton makes frequent use of **alliteration**. What effects does he achieve by this?

2 Why is the 'moon' in line 3 'blood'?

3 What is the meaning of the three verbs at the start of line 11? What effect do they have? *Hint: Think about* **onomatopoeia**, *and about any links to other stanzas.*

4 Why do you think G.K. Chesterton might have chosen this structure for his poem? *Hint: What kinds of poems are simple structures often used for, and why? Can you make any link between the structure of the poem and its meaning?*

Writing to explore, imagine and entertain

Write a story about someone who has an unexpected moment of triumph or glory.

Concentrate on exploring the person's feelings at the great moment, and the contrast between this moment and what life is usually like, rather than on telling ta long and complicated story.

Review

What did you particularly enjoy in this chapter?

What did you not like very much?

Was there anything:
- you found difficult to understand?
- you discovered or understood for the first time?

Use this checklist to help you answer these questions and to review the progress you have made.

- **You have read**: a pre-1914 poem, and one written a little later; an extract from a modern translation of the Anglo-Saxon poem, *Beowulf*; extracts from two autobiographies; one of Aesop's Fables; two pieces of non-fiction writing about a reptile found in the Far East.

- **You have thought about how writers use**: the structures of Old English poetry, such as alliteration, rhythm and kennings; modern poetic structures; language and presentational devices in information texts; different genres such as fables, heroic verse and information texts.

- **You have written to**: imagine, explore and entertain – three different kinds of narrative; inform, explain and describe – an obituary, an information sheet and a personal experience; persuade, argue and advise – a letter; analyse, review and comment – two responses to texts.

- **To improve your writing you have thought about**: word families, and the spellings of unusual and difficult words; how the meaning of words can change or vary; using words precisely, including adjectives which compare the qualities of nouns; abbreviations and contractions; achieving coherence and cohesion; humour.

- **Your speaking and listening work has included**: group discussion of ideas and issues; a presentation on the background to a text; an improvisation based on a scene from a text; evaluating your own and others' work.

- **You may have used ICT to**: research and explain technical vocabulary; research other information; spellcheck, and present final drafts of your writing neatly and attractively.